# AUTHENTIC Anglo Indian Recipes

Rishi Mendez

Published by Rishi Mendez, 2024.

RISHI

# RISHI MENDEZ

# AUTHENTIC

# INDIAN RECIPES

ANglo

While every precaution has been taken in the preparation of this book, the publisher assumes no responsibility for errors or omissions, or for damages resulting from the use of the information contained herein.

AUTHENTIC ANGLO INDIAN RECIPES

**First edition. September 18, 2024.**

Copyright © 2024 Rishi Mendez.

ISBN: 979-8227770271

Written by Rishi Mendez.

To Treza Correia, my childhood housekeeper and the heart behind our kitchen. Your culinary wisdom and true love for Anglo Indian cooking inspired this book.

Growing up in a big house, watching you cook , was always a comfort to me. The warmth of your kitchen and the delicious aromas of your dishes , filled my days with wonder . Thank you for teaching me the value of food, of home cooking tradition, and love in every ancestral dish.

This book is a tribute to you and the flavors that shaped my childhood .

Thank you for the comfort , your stories, and memories that have enriched my life.

Rishi Mendez
hellorishimendez@gmail.com

1

# DEDICATION

To Treza Correia, my childhood housekeeper and the heart behind our kitchen. Your culinary wisdom and true love for Anglo Indian cooking inspired this book.

Growing up in a big house, watching you cook , was always a comfort to me. The warmth of your kitchen and the delicious aromas of your dishes , filled my days with wonder . Thank you for teaching me the value of food, of home cooking tradition, and love in every ancestral dish. This book is a tribute to you and the flavors that shaped my childhood .

Thank you for the comfort , your stories, and memories that have enriched my life.

# Prologue

Growing up as an Anglo-Indian in a large, stately riverside home, my world was a unique blend of solitude and richness. The riverside sprawling home, surrounded by the quiet company of nature, extensive grounds with hundreds of fruit , spice and coffee trees , was alive with the sounds of two German Shepherd dogs, quacking ducks, and the gentle mooing of cows by the pond , where tadpoles abounded. The days were shaped by strict standards, a routine that echoed through the grand halls of our house. The fond memory of my grandfather pacing the extensive lawns smoking his cigar after dinner .Yet, within this structure, there was warmth—found in the comforting presence of Treza Correia, our housekeeper and the true heart of our home.

Treza's kitchen was a haven, filled with the rich aromas of spices and the sound of sizzling copper and brass pans , meal time bells and gold rimmed tableware . As a child, I often found myself gravitating toward her side, seeking solace in the rhythmic preparation of meals that filled our home with love . Then too , whenever I wanted to escape the stern look of my grandfather , or to ignore the continued absence of my parents in their careers .

I followed her everywhere , while she prepared sumptuous Anglo Indian meals , set the table , and served the food . I tagged along when she supervised workers who fed the dogs , cows and ducks . Collected peppercorns at her behest , from the creepers on which they grew , and was with her always , while she monitored day workers harvest mangoes and coconuts . I guess my eyes absorbed everything then , and stored it in my subconscious . Her talent though , was cooking , preserving and pickling . In her hands, food was more than sustenance; it was a language of care and tradition passed down through generations. She made sure everyone got their favorite food and that everyone was well fed .

' Authentic Anglo-Indian Recipes ', focuses on using readily available ingredients to create flavorful, nutritious dishes. For those ingredients that might be expensive or hard to find, readily affordable substitutions have been included , without compromising on taste. The majority of the recipes are minimalistic , ensuring simplicity without sacrificing flavor. With a special emphasis on eco friendly easy nutritious dishes, all with a clear description .

This book supports many quick , healthy eating recipes for individuals who live alone , or as a family. For those who would prefer additions to make the dishes more calorie dense , notes about the subject have been included .

These recipes, which form the core of this book, are not merely dishes , but memories—each one a connection to a proud heritage, upbringing, and warmth , enabling to experience the blend of history, tradition, and love that is the essence of Anglo-Indian cuisine.

This book is a testament that mankind can be well fed using basic , everyday ingredients providing optimum nourishment , all the important nutrients and enjoyment at every meal . You will find quick meals , fast paced dishes adapted to city life , no frills , basic , grounded in life preparations , elaborate recipes and generally varied tastes to suit every palate .

These recipes are continued down the generations by the Anglo Indian community , who are basically descended from Britain , Portugal , Spain , Denmark and France . Hence the recipes detailed here are a delightful blend of these European cultures , while incorporating a bit of the flavors of the host country .

Authentic Anglo-Indian Recipes is more than a collection of dishes; it is a testament to of cultural exchange, adaptation, and survival. From the lush greenery of the estates of Mysore , the mysteries of Calcutta , the vibrant streets of Goa , the sprawling

Anglo Indian bungalows of Edacochi , to the serene beaches and churches of Fort Kochi , Anglo-Indian cuisine has been influenced by the subcontinent's diverse regions, yet it remains distinct in its simplicity, comfort, and warmth.

Important Note : For Lactose intolerant , the milk in these recipes can be substituted with lactose free milk or a tablespoon of non dairy creamer , coconut milk , or almond milk .

For dishes requiring an oven , an air fryer can be substituted . The dishes are smart - pot friendly . You just have to adjust the timings and select the correct mode .

And of course , you can mix and match dishes from different chapters , to suit your whims and desires . You can navigate a whole life of mealtimes using this book , and still go back craving these time tested dishes , again and again .

Happy cooking !

# TABLE OF CONTENTS

## Chapters

# CHAPTER ONE
# BREAKFAST MENUS

**PANCAKE RECIPES**


**1. SWEET QUICK PANCAKES**

Preparation and cooking time 20-30 min

Level : Easy

Ingredients:

- 1 cup all-purpose flour

- 1/4 cup sugar

- 1/2 teaspoon cinnamon powder

- 1/2 teaspoon baking powder

- 1/4 teaspoon salt

- 1/2 cup milk / reconstituted milk

- 1 egg

- 2 tablespoons melted butter or ghee or olive oil

Method :

1. In a mixing bowl, combine the flour, sugar, cinnamon powder, baking powder, and salt.

2. In a separate bowl, whisk together the milk, egg, and melted butter or ghee or oil

3. Gradually add the wet ingredients to the dry ingredients, stirring until just combined. The batter should coat the spoon , be thick and fall easily

4. Heat a pan over medium heat and lightly grease it with butter or ghee or olive oil

5. Pour a medium ladleful of batter onto the pan , spread into a round shape about the dimension of a bun and cook until bubbles form on the surface. Flip and cook until golden brown.

6. Serve hot, drizzled with honey or chocolate syrup or maple syrup or just spread jam / marmalade or sprinkle one square of milk chocolate or dark chocolate cut into bits or even a dusting of fine sugar .

Note : You can top these pancakes with frozen or fresh strawberries ( optional )


## 2. BANANA CINNAMON PANCAKES

Preparation and cooking time 20-30 min

Level : Easy

Ingredients:

- 1 cup sliced and mashed ripe bananas

- 1 cup all-purpose flour

- 1/2 teaspoon cinnamon powder

- 1/2 teaspoon baking powder

- 1/4 teaspoon salt

- 1 egg

- 1/2 cup milk

- 2 tablespoons sugar

- 2 tablespoons melted butter or ghee

Method :

1. In a mixing bowl, combine the flour, cinnamon powder, baking powder, and salt.

2. In a separate bowl, whisk together the mashed bananas, egg, milk, sugar, and melted butter.

3. Add the wet ingredients to the dry ingredients and mix until just combined.

4. Heat a pan over medium heat and grease with butter or oil

5. Pour a medium ladleful of batter onto the pan, circling it into the size of a bun , by spreading it slightly.

6. Cook until bubbles form on the surface, then flip and cook until golden brown.

7. Serve with a sprinkle of fine sugar or a drizzle of maple syrup / or jam / or cream cheese spread / or fruit preserve

Note: You can top it with two slices of apple topped with a teaspoon of cream for a richer variety ( optional )


3. Rice Flour Pancakes

Preparation and cooking time 20-30 min

Level : Easy

Ingredients:

- 1 cup rice flour

- 1/4 cup grated desiccated coconut

- 1/4 teaspoon salt

- 1/2 teaspoon baking powder

- 1 egg

- 1/2 cup milk / or reconstituted milk / or coconut milk

- 1 tablespoon sugar

- 2 tablespoons melted butter or oil or ghee

Method :

1. In a mixing bowl, combine the rice flour, grated coconut, salt, and baking powder.

2. In a separate bowl, whisk together the egg, milk, sugar, and melted butter.

3. Gradually add the wet ingredients to the dry ingredients, stirring until smooth.

4. Heat a pan over medium heat and lightly grease with butter or oil .

5. Pour a spoonful of batter onto the pan and spread it out into a thin pancake size of a small tortilla .

6. Cook until edges begin to lift, then flip and cook until golden brown.

7. Serve with a drizzle of any sweet syrup / or jam / orfruit preserve / chutney .

Note: This pancake can be smeared with a little peanut butter for a nuttier option ( optional )

## 4. SAVORY ONION AND GREEN CHILI PANCAKES

Preparation and cooking time 20-30 min

Level : Easy

Ingredients:

- 1 cup chickpea flour
- 1/4 cup finely chopped onions
- 1/4 teaspoon paprika / or any curry powder / or black pepper /

- 1/2 teaspoon cumin seeds ( optional )
- 1/4 teaspoon salt
- 1/2 cup water
- 1 tablespoon oil or butter or ghee for cooking

Method :

1. In a bowl, combine chickpea flour, chopped onions, turmeric powder, curry or paprika or pepper powder , cumin seeds, if using , and salt.

2. Gradually add water and mix to form a smooth somewhat thick batter.

3. Heat a pan over medium heat and add a little oil or butter

4. Pour a ladleful of batter onto the pan, spreading it out evenly to the size of a tortilla

5. Cook until the edges begin to turn golden, then flip and cook until the other side is golden brown.

6. Serve hot with a side of plain yogurt or chutney

Note : While you flip the cooked pancake , you can break a small egg on the top with a tablespoon of water on it and cook on low heat until egg is cooked ( optional )


## 5 . COCONUT ROLLED UP PANCAKES

Preparation and cooking time 30 min

Level : Medium hard

Ingredients:


- 1 cup all-purpose flour

- 1/2 cup desiccated coconut


- 1/4 cup sugar for the batter , plus 2 tablespoons sugar for the coconut filling

- 1/2 teaspoon cinnamon powder (optional )

- 1/2 teaspoon baking powder

- 1/4 teaspoon salt

- 1/2 cup milk or reconstituted milk

- 1 egg

- 2 tablespoons melted butter or ghee or oil

Method :

1. In a mixing bowl, combine the flour, sugar, cinnamon powder, if using , baking powder, and salt.

2. In a separate bowl, whisk together the milk, egg, and melted butter or ghee or oil

3. Gradually add the wet ingredients to the dry ingredients, stirring until just combined. The batter should coat the spoon , and fall easily but not thick

4. Heat a small saucepan on low heat add three tablespoons of water , the two tablespoons of sugar and the desiccated coconut. Combine on low heat until the coconut mixture is moist and sticky

enough with the melted sugar , to fill the pancake but should not be so dry . Set aside .

5. Heat a pan over medium heat and lightly grease it with butter or ghee or olive oil

6. Pour a medium ladleful of batter onto the pan , spread into a round shape about the dimension of a tortilla and cook until bubbles form on the surface. Flip and cook until golden . Flip back and fill a teaspoonful of the coconut filling evenly in the middle . Roll up with a spatula . Slide neatly into a plate .

6. Serve hot . These pancakes can be eaten as it is , or drizzled with chocolate or fruit syrup ( optional )


## 6. OAT PANCAKES

Preparation and cooking time 45 minutes

Level : Medium hard

Ingredients:

- 1 cup rolled quick cooking oats
- 1 cup milk
- 1 large egg
- 1 tablespoon sugar
- 1/4 teaspoon salt
- 1 teaspoon baking powder
- 1/2 teaspoon cinnamon (optional)
- 1/2 teaspoon vanilla extract
- Butter or oil for cooking

Method :

1. Blend the oats dry in a blender or food processor until they become a fine flour.

2. In a bowl, mix the oat flour, sugar, salt, baking powder, and cinnamon ( if using )

3. In another bowl, whisk together the milk, egg, and vanilla extract.

4. Combine the wet and dry ingredients, stirring until just combined.

5. Heat a pan over medium heat and grease with butter or oil.

6. Pour a small amount of batter into the pan, spreading it into a circle the size of a bun

7. Cook until bubbles form on the surface, then flip and cook until golden brown.

8. Serve with jam or honey, fresh fruit, or flavored yogurt.

Note : After you flip the pancake , you can add a teaspoon of grated Parmesan cheese to each and fold it . ( optional )

# ANGLO INDIAN BREAD BASED-BREAKFASTS

## 1.  BREAD PUDDING

Preparation and cooking time 50 min
Level : Medium hard


Ingredients:
- 6 slices of day-old bread, cut into cubes
- 2 cups milk or reconstituted milk
- 2 eggs
- 1/2 cup sugar
- 1/4 cup raisins or seasonal fruit or frozen strawberries
- 1/4 cup chopped nuts (optional)
- 1 teaspoon vanilla extract
- 1/2 teaspoon cinnamon powder
- A pinch of nutmeg ( optional )
- 2 tablespoons butter, melted


Method :
1. Preheat your oven or Air fryer to 350°F (175°C).
2. Grease a baking dish or Air fryer liner and place the bread cubes in it. Sprinkle raisins and nuts if using , over the bread.
3. In a bowl, whisk together milk, eggs, sugar, vanilla extract, cinnamon, and nutmeg ( if using ) . Pour this mixture over the bread cubes, carefully pressing down with a spoon to soak the bread well so it does not seep out of the liner
4. Drizzle the melted butter over the top.

5. Bake ( or air fry ) for 30-35 minutes, at 180 degrees C or until the pudding is golden and set. If using an Air fryer check the pudding at 25 min , as it may be done by then .

6. Serve warm, either plain or with a dollop of breakfast cream ( optional ) or even just fruit jam or a dusting of powdered sugar.

Note : This pudding can be baked with a tablespoon shredded cheddar or grated Parmesan half way through baking for those who love cheese flavors (optional )

## 2. BREAD UPMA

Preparation and Cooking time 20 min
Level : Easy

Ingredients:
- 6 slices of bread, cut into small cubes
- 1 onion, finely chopped

- 1 tomato, chopped with small strip of bell pepper ( optional )

- 1/2 a teaspoon mustard seeds

- 1/2 teaspoon black pepper powder

- 1/2 teaspoon curry powder
- A handful of cilantro or parsley leaves or green onion shoots or a pinch of dried herbs
- 2 tablespoons oil or ghee or butter
- Salt, to taste

- Fresh cilantro leaves, chopped for garnish or a pinch of dried herbs

- Lemon juice, to taste


Method :

1.  Heat oil or ghee in a pan. Add mustard seeds, and when they begin to splutter, add cilantro / parsley leaves / or a pinch of dried herbs .

2. Add onions immediately and sauté until the onions are golden brown.

3. Add the tomatoes and bell pepper if using and curry powder, and cook until the tomatoes are soft.

4. Add the bread cubes and salt. Mix well and cook for a few minutes in low heat until the bread absorbs the flavors and turns slightly crispy.

5. Garnish with fresh cilantro or parsley leaves or a pinch more of dried herbs and a squeeze of lemon juice. Serve hot.

Note : This dish can be topped with a teaspoon of grated Parmesan cheese , while still hot ( optional )

## 3. SIMPLE FRENCH TOAST
Preparation and cooking time 30 min
Level : Easy


Ingredients:
  - 4 slices of bread
  - 2 eggs
  - 1/2 cup milk or reconstituted milk
  - 1 or 2 tablespoon sugar
  - 1/2 teaspoon vanilla extract
  - 1/4 teaspoon cinnamon powder (optional)
  - A pinch of salt
  - Butter or oil or ghee for frying

  - Maple syrup, honey, chocolate spread or powdered sugar for serving


Method :

1. In a bowl, whisk together eggs, milk, sugar, vanilla extract, cinnamon powder (if using), and salt.

2. Heat a skillet or frying pan over medium heat and add a little butter or oil.

3. Dip each bread slice into the egg mixture, ensuring both sides are saturated and coated, then place it in the hot pan.

4. Cook until golden brown on both sides, on low heat about 2-3 minutes per side.

5. Serve hot with syrup, or honey, or jam or even a sprinkle of powdered sugar.

Note : Sprinkle grated Parmesan cheese on top while still hot , if you prefer a cheesy version ( optional )

## 4. FRIED SPICED BREAD

Preparation and cooking time 30 min
Level : Easy

Ingredients:
- 4 slices of bread, cut into triangles or halves

- 2 eggs

- 1 small onion, finely chopped

- A pinch of garlic powder ( optional)

- 1 green chili , finely chopped ( optional )
- A handful of fresh cilantro or parsley leaves, chopped or substitute it with a good pinch of dried herbs
- 1/4 teaspoon curry powder or Garam masala
- Salt and pepper, to taste
- 2 tablespoons oil or ghee or butter.

Method :
1. In a bowl, beat the eggs and add chopped onions, green chili ( if using ) , cilantro or parsley leaves, or dried herbs , curry powder, garlic powder, ( if using ) , salt, and pepper. Mix well.
2. Heat oil or ghee in a pan or skillet over medium heat.
3. Dip each bread slice into the egg mixture, ensuring it's saturated and well-coated with the spiced egg mix.
4. Place the coated bread slices in the hot pan and fry until golden brown on low heat until crisp on both sides.
5. Serve hot with a side of ketchup or chutney .

Note . Grated Parmesan cheese may be added ( to the batter ) , for those who prefer it . ( Optional )

## RICE AND EGG BASED BREAKFASTS

### 1. HOPPERS (Appam)

Preparation time needs ferment overnight ,
cooking time 30 min
Level : Medium hard .

Ingredients:
- 1 cup raw rice
- 1/2 cup grated desiccated or fresh coconut
- 1/2 teaspoon yeast
- 1 teaspoon sugar
- 1/2 teaspoon salt
- 1 cup milk or reconstituted milk or coconut milk
- Water as needed

Method :

1. Soak the rice in water for 4-5 hours. Drain and grind with grated coconut into a smooth batter.

2. Dissolve the yeast and sugar in warm water and let it froth. Add this to the rice batter.

3. Stir in milk or coconut milk and salt. The batter should be of pouring consistency. Let it ferment for 8 hours or overnight.

4. Heat an appam pan ( a pan with a depression in the middle ) or a small wok, pour a ladleful of batter, and swirl it around to coat the sides. Cover and cook until the edges are crisp and the center is soft.

5. Serve hot with coconut chutney or curry of your choice .

Note : There is a separate section on Anglo Indian curries and stews , For this who need it to pair it with this recipe .

Note : While the hoppers cook covered , break a small egg into the center of the hopper after the batter has set . Cook covered , another two minutes to set the egg . ( Optional )

## 2. KEDGEREE (Fish with Rice and Eggs) Fusion dish .
Preparation and cooking time 35 min
Level : Medium hard

Ingredients:
- 1 cup basmati rice , rinsed
- 200g any chunky or smoked boneless fish or canned boneless fish (like tuna , haddock or mackerel), flaked
- 2 boiled eggs, quartered
- 1 onion, finely chopped
- 2 tablespoons butter or ghee or oil
- 1 level teaspoon curry powder
- 1/4 teaspoon garlic powder or two cloves garlic
- 1pinch of ginger powder ( optional )
- Salt, to taste
- Fresh cilantro or parsley leaves, chopped , or dried herbs for garnish
- Lemon wedges for serving

Method :
1. Cook the rice in salted water until tender. Drain and set aside. Alternatively use a rice cooker with timer .

2. In a large pan, melt the butter and add the onions, and garlic. Sauté until the onions are golden.

3. Add curry powder, lower the heat and stir for a minute.

4. Add the flaked fish and cooked rice, and mix well. Cook for a few minutes until heated through.

5. Garnish with boiled eggs and fresh cilantro or parsley or just a pinch of dried herbs . Serve with lemon wedges or pickles .

Note : This dish can be served with additional eggs ( fried ) if desired ( optional )

## 3. EGG VINDALOO

Preparation and Cooking time 30 min

Level: Easy

Ingredients:

- 4 eggs, boiled and peeled
- 1 onion, finely chopped
- 2 tomatoes, chopped
- 1/2 teaspoon garlic powder
- 1 teaspoon ginger powder ( optional)
- 1 level teaspoon curry powder
- 1 level teaspoon chili or paprika powder
- 1 teaspoon vinegar
- 1 teaspoonful sugar
- 1/2 teaspoon turmeric powder
- 1/2 teaspoon herbs or a tablespoon of chopped cilantro or parsley for garnish
- 2 tablespoons oil or butter
- Salt, to taste

Method :

1.  Heat oil in a pan and add onions and sauté until golden brown.

2. Add the garlic and curry and garlic powders , ginger powder if using , and sauté low heat for just ten seconds .

3. Add the chopped tomatoes in and cook until soft.

4. Add vinegar, sugar, and salt. Cook low heat until the oil separates from the mixture

5. Add the boiled eggs and gently stir to coat them with the mix . Cook for a few more minutes.

6. Garnish with fresh cilantro or parsley leaves or dried herbs and serve with toast , warm rolls , or any type of flatbread , pita bread or tortillas .

## 4. SAUSAGE PULAO
Preparation and Cooking time 35 min
Level : Medium hard

Ingredients:
- 200g beef or chicken osausages, sliced
- 1 cup basmati rice, rinsed
- 1 onion, finely sliced
- 1 tomato, chopped
- 2 green chilies, or a quarter of bell pepper ( optional)
- 1/4 teaspoon turmeric powder
- 1/2 teaspoon garlic powder
- 1/2 teaspoon garam masala or curry powder
- 1 tablespoon oil or butter
- 2 cups water
- Salt, to taste
- Fresh cilantro or parsley leaves or dried herbs for garnish

Method :

1. Heat oil in a pan and add onions and sauté until golden.

2. Add the sausages and cook until they are browned.

3. Add tomatoes, green chilies or bell peppers ( if using )
Curry powder , garlic powder , and salt. Cook until the tomatoes are soft.

4. Add the rinsed rice and stir for a couple of minutes to coat the rice with the spices.

5. Add the two cups of water and bring to a boil. Lower the heat, cover, and cook until the rice is done. This takes approximately 12

mins in low heat after water boils . The rice should have absorbed all the water by then .

6. Sprinkle with fresh cilantro or parsley leaves or a pinch of dried herbs . Serve hot with a fried egg on top of each serving .

This dish can be prepared in the rice cooker or smart cooker using sauté mode first then the rice cook mode with timer .

These dishes represent the unique blend of Indian and British culinary traditions, offering a variety of flavors and textures perfect for breakfast.

These easy recipes offer a delicious and satisfying start to the day, combining the familiar comfort of pancakes , and bread , rice and eggs with unique Anglo-Indian flavors.

# CHAPTER TWO
# MID MORNING SNACKS
# 1. FISH CUTLETS

Preparation and cooking time: 45 minutes

Level : Medium hard

Ingredients:

- 250g boneless fish fillets (like mackerel, cod, or tuna)

- 1 large potato, boiled and mashed

- 1 small onion, chopped small


- A small piece of bell pepper chopped ( optional )


- 1 teaspoon ginger-garlic paste or 1/2 a teaspoon each of their powder

- 1/2 teaspoon turmeric powder

- 1/2 teaspoon garam masala

- 1/4 teaspoon pepper powder

- 1/2 cup breadcrumbs

- 1 egg, beaten

- Salt to taste

- Oil for frying

Method :

1. Boil or steam the fish fillets until cooked through. Around fifteen minutes. Boil the potato . Once cool , Skin and mash it . Cool and flake the fish, making sure to remove any bones. Both should not have water

2. In a bowl, mix the flaked fish with the mashed potatoes, chopped onions, bell pepper if using , ginger-garlic paste, or its powder , turmeric powder, garam masala, pepper, and salt.

- Combine everything well to form a thick mixture.

3. Take small portions of the mixture size of a lemon and shape them into round or oval patties.

4. Dip each patty in the beaten egg and then coat it with breadcrumbs.

5. Heat oil in a pan over medium heat. Shallow fry the cutlets until golden brown on both sides. Remove and drain on paper towels.

6. Serve the fish cutlets hot with ketchup or a side of chutney.

Note : Home made breadcrumbs can be made by toasting 2 slices of a day old bread in the toaster on level 3 or 4 . When cool , pulse it in a small dry food or spice grinder for half a minute .

# 2. VEGETABLE CUTLETS Fusion dish

Preparation and cooking time 45 min

Level : Medium hard

Ingredients:

- 1 cup chickpea flour known as besan
- 1/4 cup rice flour (optional, for extra crispness)
- 1/2 teaspoon turmeric powder
- 1/2 teaspoon chili powder or paprika
- 1/4 cup of chopped fresh or frozen cabbage
- 1/2 teaspoon baking soda
- Salt to taste
- 1 small onion, thinly sliced

- 1 small cooked potato ( optional )
- 2 tablespoons of frozen thawed green peas

- 1 small carrot, grated
- 1/2 cup spinach, chopped small
- 1/4 cup water (adjust this as needed)
- Oil for deep frying

Method :

1. Prepare the Batter by combining in a large mixing bowl, the chickpea flour, rice flour, if using , turmeric powder, chili powder or paprika , baking soda, and salt . Gradually add water to form a thick batter.

2. Add the Vegetables . Mix in the sliced onion, potato, if using , grated carrot, cabbage and chopped spinach until the vegetables are well coated with the batter. This batter should be thick and fall from the spoon slowly .

3. Heat oil one can deep in a deep frying pan and fry the cutlets over medium heat by dropping spoonfuls of the vegetable batter

into the hot oil. Fry them until the cutlets are golden brown and crispy on all sides, turning them occasionally.

4. Remove the cutlets with a slotted spoon and drain on paper towels. Serve hot with chutney or ketchup.


## 3. PRAWN CUTLETS

Preparation and cooking time 45 minutes

Level : Medium hard

Ingredients:

- 250g prawns, cleaned and minced or finely chopped

- 1 onion, finely chopped

- 1 green chili, finely chopped , deseeded ( optional )

- 1-inch piece of ginger, minced or 1/2 teaspoon of its powder

- 2 garlic cloves, minced or 1/2 teaspoon of its powder

- 1/2 teaspoon turmeric powder

- 1/2 teaspoon garam masala powder

- 1 medium boiled potato, mashed

- Salt and pepper, to taste

- 1 egg, beaten

- Breadcrumbs for coating

- Oil for frying

- Fresh cilantro or parsley leaves, chopped or a ouch of dried herbs

Method:

1. In a non stick pan, heat a little oil and sauté the onions, green chili if using , ginger, and garlic until golden.

2. Add the minced prawns, turmeric, and garam masala. Add half cup of warm water. Cook until the prawns are done and the mixture is dry.

3. Mix the prawn mixture with the mashed potato, fresh cilantro or dried herbs , salt, and pepper. Shape and press them into small cutlets.

4. Dip each cutlet into the beaten egg, then coat with breadcrumbs.

5. Shallow fry in just a 1/2 centimeter of hot oil until golden brown on both sides.

6. Drain on paper towels . Serve hot with a squeeze of lemon ( optional ) and some ketchup or chutney as your preference.

## 4. FISH CROQUETTES

Preparation and cooking time 45 minutes

Level : Medium hard

Ingredients:

- 250g (cooked) boneless fish (like cod , mackerel or tuna ), flaked

- 1 potato, boiled and mashed

- 1 onion, finely chopped

- 1 green chili, deseeded chopped ( optional )

- 1 teaspoon ginger-garlic paste or 1/2 teaspoon each of their powder

- 1/2 teaspoon turmeric powder

- 1/2 teaspoon black pepper powder

- 1/2 teaspoon garam masala powder ( optional )

- Salt, to taste

- 1 egg, beaten

- Breadcrumbs for coating

- Oil for frying

- Fresh cilantro or parsley leaves, chopped , or a pinch of dried herbs

- Method

1. In a pan, heat some oil and sauté the onions, green chili, if using and ginger-garlic paste or their powders , until fragrant.

2. Add the turmeric, pepper, and garam masala powders, and mix well.

3. Add the flaked fish and mashed potato to the pan, mixing thoroughly. Adjust salt.

4. Shape the mixture into small croquettes or cylindrical shapes.

5. Dip each croquette into the beaten egg, then roll in breadcrumbs to coat.

6. Deep fry or shallow fry until golden and crisp.

7. Serve with tartar sauce or ketchup or a hot sauce or yoghurt dip .

These Anglo-Indian fritters are perfect for tea-time snacks or as appetizers, offering a blend of traditional flavors with a crispy texture.

# CHAPTER THREE
# SOUPS AND STEWS

Anglo-Indian soup recipes that blend Indian flavors with British culinary traditions:


1.  Mulligatawny Soup

**Preparation and Cooking time 30 min**
Level : Easy
Mulligatawny, a popular Anglo-Indian soup, is a rich and spicy broth made with chicken, vegetables, and rice. The name of this soup is a fusion word .


Ingredients:
- 2 tbsp vegetable oil
- 1 onion, finely chopped

- 2 garlic cloves, minced

- 1 inch piece of ginger, grated or a half teaspoon of ginger powder

- 1 tsp turmeric powder

- 1 tsp coriander powder
- 1/2 tsp garam masala
- 1/2 tsp paprika (optional)
- 1 apple, peeled and chopped
- 1 carrot, skinned and chopped

- 1/2 cup cooked chicken or 100 grams of mince (optional)
- 4 cups chicken or vegetable broth
- 1/2 cup milk or reconstituted milk or coconut milk
- Salt and pepper to taste
- Cooked or steamed rice (for serving)
- Fresh cilantro leaves or a pinch of dried herbs for garnish

Method :

1. Heat oil in a large pot over medium heat. Add the onion, garlic, and ginger, and sauté until soft.

2. Stir in the turmeric, coriander, garam masala, and paprika powder, and cook for another minute.

3. Add the apple and carrot, and cook for 5 minutes.

4. Pour in the broth and bring to a boil. Reduce the heat and simmer for 15 minutes.

5. If using chicken or mince add it now. Stir in the milk or coconut milk and cook for another 15 minutes.

6. Season with salt and pepper. Serve hot with a spoonful of cooked rice and garnish with fresh cilantro leaves or a pinch of dried herbs .

Note : This soup can be topped with a teaspoon of grated Cheddar or Parmesan cheese before serving ( optional )

## 2. CALCUTTA TOMATO SOUP

**Preparation and Cooking time 30 min**

**Level : Medium hard**

This classic soup combines the tanginess of tomatoes with the richness of cream, inspired by the British influence in India .

Ingredients:
- 4 large tomatoes, chopped
- 1 onion, chopped
- 2 garlic cloves, minced or half a teaspoon level garlic powder
- 1 tbsp butter
- 1 bay leaf ( optional )
- 1/2 teaspoon sugar
- 1/4 teaspoon black pepper
- 1/4 teaspoon paprika

- 3 cups vegetable broth

- 1/2 cup heavy cream
- Salt to taste
- Fresh parsley leaves or a pinch of dried herbs for garnish

Method :

1. In a large pot, melt the butter over medium heat. Add the onion, garlic, and bay leaf, if using , and sauté until the onion is translucent.

2. Add the chopped tomatoes, sugar, black pepper, and paprika. Cook for 10 minutes, stirring occasionally.

3. Pour in the vegetable broth and bring to a boil. Reduce the heat and simmer for 15 minutes.

4. Remove the bay leaf, cool it for 20 min then blend the soup until smooth using an immersion hand blender or in batches in a regular blender.

5. Return the soup to the pot, stir in the cream, and season with salt. Heat through but do not boil.

6. Serve hot, garnished with fresh parsley leaves or a pinch of dried herbs .

## 3. THIN PEPPER SOUP

Preparation and cooking time 25 min

Level : Easy

Pepper Soup , is a tangy and spicy soup that is perfect for aiding digestion.

Ingredients:
- 1/4 cup tamarind pulp ( can be store bought )
- 2 cups water
- 2 tomatoes, chopped
- 1 teaspoon mustard seeds ( optional )
- 1/2 tsp black pepper
- 1/2 teaspoon turmeric powder
- 1 tablespoon oil
- 2 garlic cloves, crushed or 1/2 teaspoon garlic powder
- 1/2 tsp asafoetida powder (hing)
- Salt to taste
- Fresh cilantro leaves or a pinch of dried herbs for garnish

Method :

1. Soak the tamarind pulp in 2 cups of water for 15 minutes, then strain and set aside.

2. Heat oil in a pan over medium heat. Add mustard seeds . If using . When they pop , and crushed garlic. Sauté for ten seconds

3. Add the chopped tomatoes and cook until soft.

4. Pour in the tamarind water, and add turmeric powder, black pepper, and salt. Bring to a boil, then reduce the heat and simmer for 10 minutes.

5. Add asafoetida and stir well. Garnish with fresh cilantro leaves or the dried herbs, and serve hot. This is mainly a thin soup used for digestive purposes.


## 4. CHICKEN SOUP

Preparation and Cooking time 35 min
Level : Medium hard


A hearty chicken soup with a touch of Indian spices, this recipe is comforting and flavorful.

Ingredients:

- 2 tbsp vegetable oil or butter

- 1 onion, chopped

- 2 garlic cloves, minced or 1/2 teaspoon of garlic powder
- 1 inch piece of ginger, grated or 1/2 teaspoon of ginger powder
- 1/2 teaspoon turmeric powder
- 1/2 teaspoon curry powder

- 1/4 tsp cinnamon powder
- 1/4 tsp black pepper
- 2 chicken breasts, diced
- 4 cups chicken broth ( you can use broth cubes )
- 1/2 cup milk or reconstituted milk or coconut milk
- 1 carrot, chopped
- 1 potato, chopped
- 1/2 cup green peas
- Salt to taste , if using broth cubes it will already have salt
- Fresh cilantro leaves or a pinch of dried herbs for garnish

Method :

1. Sauté the onion with garlic until translucent.

1. Add all dry spices sauté ten seconds and add chicken cubes. Stir fry for two minutes.

1. Add the milk and stock , potato cubes , peas and carrot cubed . Cook on medium for twenty minutes until creamy .

1. Serve with toasted bread , warm rolls , or flat bread .

## 5. PUMPKIN SOUP
Preparation and cooking time 45 min
Level : Medium hard


Ingredients:
- 500 grams pumpkin, peeled and chopped
- 1 large onion, finely chopped
- 2 cloves garlic, minced or 1/2 teaspoon of garlic powder
- 1 /2 teaspoon ginger powder ( optional )
- 1 large tomato, chopped
- 1/2 teaspoon turmeric powder
- 1/2 teaspoon paprika or red chili powder
- 1/2 teaspoon garam masala
- 1/4 cup milk or reconstituted milk or coconut milk
- 4 cups vegetable broth or water
- Salt to taste
- Oil or butter
- Fresh cilantro leaves or a pinch of dried herbs for garnish


Method:

1. Heat oil in a large pot. Add chopped onions and cook until translucent. Stir in garlic and ginger , if using , cooking them until aromatic.

2. Add chopped tomatoes, turmeric powder, paprika or red chili powder, and salt. Cook in low heat until the tomatoes soften and the oil or butter begins to separate.

3. Add chopped pumpkin and stir well. Pour in vegetable broth or water and bring to a boil. Reduce heat and simmer until the pumpkin is tender, about 20 minutes.

4. Cool it for twenty minutes. Use an immersion blender to blend the soup until smooth. Alternatively, you can blend in batches using a countertop blender.

5. Stir in milk or coconut milk and garam masala. Adjust seasoning if necessary.

6. Garnish with fresh cilantro leaves or a pinch of dried herbs and serve hot with warm rolls or lightly toasted bread .

## 6. BEEF STEW WITH POTATOES :

Preparation and marinade : 1 hour , cooking time 30 minutes if pressure cooked , or 1.5 hours if normal pot cooked .

Level : Medium hard

Ingredients:

- 500g beef, cut into cubes
- 2 large potatoes, peeled and cut into quarters
- 2 onions, sliced thinly
- 2 tomatoes, chopped
- 2 carrots, sliced
- 1-inch piece of ginger, minced , or 1/2 teaspoon of ginger powder or paste
- 4-5 garlic cloves, minced or 1/2 teaspoon of garlic powder or paste
- 2 green chilies deseeded ( optional )
- 1 bay leaf ( optional )
- 1 cinnamon stick
- 4-5 cloves
- 4-5 peppercorns
- 1 teaspoon curry powder

- 1 teaspoon turmeric powder
- 1 teaspoon pepper powder
- 1/2 teaspoon garam masala powder
- Salt, to taste
- 2 tablespoons oil or ghee
- 4 cups water
- Fresh cilantro or parsley leaves for garnish or a pinch of dried herbs

METHOD :

1. Marinate the Beef:

- In a bowl, mix the beef with turmeric, curry , and pepper powders. Set aside for 30 minutes.

2. In a heavy-bottomed pan or pressure cooker, heat the oil or ghee. Add the bay leaf, if using , and cinnamon stick, cloves, and peppercorns, and sauté for a minute until fragrant.

3 . Add the sliced onions and green chilies if using . Sauté until the onions turn golden brown.

4. Add the minced ginger and garlic and sauté for another two minutes until the raw smell disappears. If using powder , sauté only ten seconds

5. Add the marinated beef to the pot and cook on medium heat until the meat is browned on all sides.

6. Stir in the chopped tomatoes and cook until they soften. Add the potato quarters and carrots.

7. Pour in 4 cups of water. Add salt to taste and stir well. Bring the stew to a boil, then reduce the heat to low, cover, and let it simmer for 1.5 to 2 hours until the beef is tender. (If using a pressure cooker, cook for about 20-25 minutes after the first whistle.)

8. Once the beef is tender and the potatoes are cooked, sprinkle the garam masala over the stew and stir well.

9. Garnish with fresh cilantro or parsley leaves or a pinch of dried herbs . Serve hot with steamed rice , warm bun , flatbread or lightly toasted bread .


## 7. KALE or SPINACH SOUP WITH SAUSAGES

Preparation and Cooking time 25 min

Level : Easy

Ingredients:

- 1 large onion, chopped
- 2 garlic cloves, minced or 1/2 teaspoon of garlic powder
- 2 tablespoons olive oil or butter
- 4 medium potatoes, peeled and diced
- 1 liter (4 cups) chicken or vegetable broth either from cubes or home made
- 200g chorizo or smoked or canned or frozen sausage, sliced
- 100g kale, or spinach leaves thinly sliced
- Salt and pepper to taste

Method :

1. Heat a casserole on medium heat , add butter or oil and sauté the onions until translucent. Add the garlic and vegetable stock .

1. When it comes to a boil reduce heat and add the diced potatoes , kale and sliced sausages . Adjust the salt if the sausage is salted already .

1. Cook until potatoes and sausages are done . Add ground pepper to taste . This is a medium thin and very satisfying Anglo Indian soup .

Note : A cup of milk may be added for those who like the soup creamy . Alternatively, a teaspoon of grated Parmesan cheese may be sprinkled for added flavor ( optional )


## 8. TROTTERS SOUP (PAYA SOUP):

Preparation and cooking time 3 hours
Level : Hard
- Ingredients:
- 2 Trotters (goat or lamb)
- 2 onions chopped
- 1 teaspoon of ginger-garlic paste, or 1/2 a teaspoon each of their powder
- 1/2 a teaspoon of turmeric

- 4 Cloves , a stick of cinnamon
- 2 Bayleaves ( optional )
- A sprig of cilantro or parsley leaves, or a pinch of dried herbs
- 1 teaspoon of lemon juice
- Salt and pepper to taste
- 2 tablespoons of oil or a tablespoon of butter
- A cup of milk or reconstituted milk

-

- Method:
    1. Clean the trotters thoroughly.
    2. In a large pot, heat oil and add cloves, cinnamon, and bay leaves, if using , sautéing until aromatic.
    3. Add chopped onions and cook until golden, then add ginger-garlic paste or its powder and cook for a minute .

4. Add the cleaned trotters, turmeric, salt, and black pepper, stirring well.

5. Add enough water to cover the trotters, bring to a boil, then reduce heat and simmer and slow cook for three or more hours until the trotters are tender and the broth is flavorful .

6. Adjust seasoning, add a squeeze of lemon juice, and garnish with chopped cilantro or parsley leaves or a pinch of dried herbs . Turn off the heat and add the cup of milk .

7. Serve hot, often enjoyed as a nourishing soup on its own in cold or rainy months or as a side with lightly toasted bread , buns or steamed or cooked rice.

## 9. MULTI VEGETABLE SOUP

Preparation and cooking time 45 minutes

Level : Medium hard

Ingredients:

- 1 cup carrots, diced
- 1 cup potatoes, diced
- 1 cup beans, chopped
- 1 cup peas
- 1 cup canned or frozen corn kernels ( optional )
- 1 large onion, finely chopped
- 2 tomatoes, chopped
- 2 cloves garlic, minced or 1/2 a teaspoon of its powder
- 1-inch piece ginger, minced or 1/2 a teaspoon of its powder
- 1-2 green chilies, deseeded chopped ( optional )
- 1 teaspoon curry powder
- 1/2 teaspoon turmeric powder
- 1/2 teaspoon garam masala
- 1 bay leaf ( optional )
- 4 cups vegetable broth from store bought cubes or water .

- 2 tablespoons oil or butter
- Salt and pepper to taste . Adjust salt if using broth cubes as they come salted .

   - Fresh cilantro or parsley leaves or a pinch of dried herbs
   for garnish
   - A cup of milk or reconstituted milk or coconut milk .

Method:
1. Clean and chop all the vegetables into uniform pieces.
2. Heat oil or butter in a large pot. Add bay leaf. If using . After a minute add chopped onions, garlic, ginger, and green chilies if using . Sauté until the onions are translucent.
3. Stir in curry powder, turmeric powder, and salt. Cook for a minute before adding the chopped tomatoes. Cook until the tomatoes are softened and the oil starts to separate.
4. Cook Vegetables in the pot . Add the diced carrots, potatoes, beans, peas, and corn if using , to the pot. Stir well to coat with the spices.
5. Pour in the vegetable broth or water. Bring to a boil, then reduce the heat adjust the salt and pepper and let it simmer until the vegetables are tender (about 25 minutes).
6. Finish the Soup by adding garam masala and adjust seasoning if needed. Let the soup simmer for another 5 minutes. Turn off the heat and add the cup of milk .
7. Garnish and Serve: Garnish with fresh cilantro or parsley leaves or the pinch of dried herbs and serve hot with steamed or cooked rice , bun , flatbread , or lightly toasted bread .

This soup is hearty and flavorful, incorporating a variety of vegetables and spices typical of Anglo-Indian cuisine.

10. CHICKEN STEW

Preparation and cooking time 45 minutes

Level : Medium hard

Ingredients:
- Chicken thighs or chicken drumsticks 500 grams
- 1 cup Milk or reconstituted milk or coconut milk
- 1 large potato
- 1 large carrot
- 1/2 cup frozen or canned green peas
- 1 onion chopped
- 1 piece of cinnamon
- 4 cloves
- 1 teaspoon garam masala
- Salt and pepper to taste
- 1 tablespoon level all purpose flour
- 2 tablespoons oil or butter
- 1 cube chicken stock ( It contains salt )

- 2 sprigs cilantro or parsley or a pinch dried herbs

Method :

1. Heat oil in a large pot over medium heat. Add the onion, garlic, and ginger, and sauté until soft. Add the cinnamon stick and cloves

2. Stir in garam masala , salt and black pepper. Cook for another minute.

3. Add the chicken and cook on low heat for ten minutes until browned on all sides.

4. Pour in two cups of water , dissolve the spoon of flour in three tablespoons of warm water and add it to the pot with the crumbled chicken broth cube , add the carrot and potato, and bring to a boil.

5. Reduce the heat to low and simmer for 25 minutes until the vegetables are tender stirring every five minutes. The sauce will be thick and creamy .

6. Stir in the milk or coconut milk and green peas. Cook for another 5 minutes.

7. Check the salt , sprinkle with a bit of pepper and garnish with fresh cilantro or parsley leaves or a pinch of the dried herbs . Serve hot with flat bread , warm rolls , or hoppers called ' appam ' . Recipe of hoppers is included in the breakfast chapter .

This stew reflects the fusion of Indian spices with British culinary practices, resulting in unique and flavorful dishes. Enjoy them as a comforting main course!


## 11. CREAMY EGG STEW

Preparation and cooking time 45 minutes
Level : Easy
Ingredients :

- 4 hard boiled eggs

- 2 cups of milk or reconstituted milk or coconut milk

- 1 onion chopped

- 1 tomato chopped or 1 tablespoon of tomato paste / sauce

- 1 tablespoon lemon juice or vinegar

- 1 boiled potato

- 1 sliced steamed carrot . ( Steam manually or Slice and steam In microwave for 2 minutes with 2 tablespoons water )

- 1 piece of cinnamon or 1/2 teaspoon of its powder

- 4 cloves or 1/4 teaspoon of its powder

- 1 level teaspoon black pepper

- 1 level teaspoon of curry powder

- 2 sprigs if cilantro or parsley chopped or 2 pinch of dried herbs

- 4 clove chopped garlic or 1/2 teaspoon of its powder

- 2 tablespoon oil or butter

Method :

1. Heat the oil in a medium casserole and sauté the onions with cloves and cinnamon or their powders , until translucent

2. Add the curry powder , tomato or tomato paste ,herbs , garlic and pepper . Sauté for a minute

3. Add the boiled cubed potato and steamed carrot and the cups of milk and gently bring it to a boil on low heat

4. Add the boiled peeled and halved eggs gently . Simmer until sauce is thick . Turn off the heat and add the lemon juice or vinegar after five minutes.

5. Serve with warm rolls , bun , flatbread or lightly toasted bread or naan .

## 12. LENTIL SOUP

Preparation and cooking time 45 min

Level : Medium hard

Ingredients:

- 1 cup split red lentils or yellow lentils

- 1 medium onion, finely chopped

- 2 cloves garlic, minced or 1/2 teaspoon of its powder

- 1 small tomato, chopped

- 1 carrot, chopped (optional)

- 1 teaspoon tomato paste or sauce

- ½ teaspoon turmeric powder

- ½ teaspoon black pepper

- 1 tablespoon butter , ghee , or oil

- Salt to taste

- Fresh cilantro / parsley leaves for garnish or a pinch of chopped herbs

- 1 tablespoon lemon juice

Method:

1. Prepare Lentils by washing the lentils thoroughly under running water several times . Drain .

2. Cook the washed Lentils in a large pot, with about 4 cups of water, turmeric powder, and salt. Bring it to a boil, then reduce the heat and simmer until the lentils are soft and cooked (around 30 minutes). You can use a pressure cooker for faster results with washed lentils , only two cups of water , turmeric and salt . The lentils then will be ready in 5 minutes after the first whistle .

3. Make the Tempering by heating butter or oil or ghee In a separate pan, heat the ghee or oil. Add the chopped onion and garlic, or its powder sautéing until they turn golden.

4. Add Vegetables , the chopped tomato, carrot, and cook for 4-5 minutes until the tomato softens and is like a purée

5. Combine and Season by pouring the tempering onion and vegetable mixture into the cooked lentils. Stir well and adjust the consistency by adding more water if needed. Add freshly ground black pepper , and adjust salt to taste.

6. Simmer: Let the soup simmer for another 5-10 minutes to let the flavors combine together.

7. Finish by stirring in the lemon juice, garnish with fresh cilantro or parsley chopped or the pinch of dried herbs and serve hot with warm bread , flatbread or steamed or cooked rice.

Note : For those who prefer a creamier lentil soup, cool the soup to room temperature and blend until smooth in a blender and return to the pan to reheat it .

A teaspoonful of grated Parmesan may be added (optional)

This Anglo-Indian lentil soup is both nourishing and flavorful, combining the warmth of Indian spices with a hearty, simple lentil base.

## 13. POTATO SOUP

Preparation and cooking time 45 minutes

Level : Medium hard

Ingredients:

- 4 medium potatoes, peeled and diced
- 1 large onion, finely chopped
- 3 cloves garlic, minced or 1/2 teaspoon of its powder
- 1 tsp ginger paste or 1/4 teaspoon of its powder (optional)
- 4 cups vegetable or chicken stock

- 1 cup milk or reconstituted milk or coconut milk for a richer flavor
- 2 tablespoons butter or oil

- 1 teaspoon of tomato paste or tomato sauce
- 1/2 teaspoon black pepper
- Salt to taste

- Fresh cilantro or parsley leaves, chopped or a pinch of dried herbs

- A tablespoon of lemon juice

Method :

1. Heat butter or oil in a large pot. Lower the heat

2. Add onions and garlic (and ginger, if using). Sauté until softened and slightly golden.

3. Add the diced potatoes and sauté for another 2-3 minutes, allowing them to coat in the flavors.

4. Pour in the stock and bring the mixture to a boil. The stock may have salt . So adjust salt accordingly. Once boiling, reduce the heat and let it simmer for about 25 minutes, or until the potatoes are tender.

5. Cool the soup to room temperature .Blend the soup using a hand blender or by transferring it in batches to a blender, until smooth.

6. Stir in the milk or coconut milk and let the soup simmer for another 5 minutes. Add salt and pepper to taste.

7. Serve hot, garnished with fresh cilantro or parsley or a pinch of dried herbs and the lemon juice if desired.

This potato soup is creamy, flavorful, and simple to prepare with easy-to-find ingredients. You could also add a sprinkle of grated Parmesan cheese to make it richer, but this version works perfectly too .

## 14. FARMERS SOUP

Preparation and cooking time 45 minutes

Level : Medium hard

This soup will be featuring potatoes, carrots, sausages, milk, and green peas . It is a hearty and nutritious meal in itself .

Ingredients:

- 2 medium potatoes, diced
- 2 medium carrots, sliced
- 1 cup green peas ( canned or frozen)
- 4 sausages (any kind , beef pork or chicken), sliced
- 2 cups milk or reconstituted milk or coconut milk
- 1 cup vegetable or chicken broth
- 1 tablespoon butter or oil
- 1 onion, chopped

- 2 cloves garlic, minced or 1/2 teaspoon of its powder
- A tablespoon of tomato paste or tomato sauce
- Salt and pepper, to taste
- A pinch of cinnamon powder ( optional )

- Fresh cilantro / parsley chopped , or a pinch of dried herbs
Method :

1. Prepare the soup base by heating butter or oil in a large pot over medium heat. Sauté the onions and garlic until soft and fragrant.

2. Add the diced potatoes, carrots, and green peas. Sauté for a couple of minutes.

3. Add the sliced sausages to the pot. Cook until they are slightly browned.

4. Pour in the broth, cover the pot, and let it simmer for 20 minutes, until the vegetables are tender. Check salt as broth contains salt .

5. Once the vegetables are cooked, stir in the milk. Add salt, pepper, tomato paste or sauce and a pinch of cinnamon , if using. Let the soup gently simmer for another 15 minutes, stirring occasionally , taking care not to burn

6. Adjust seasoning to taste. Add the chopped or dried herbs .Ladle the soup into bowls and serve with warm rolls , bun , lightly toasted bread or flatbread .

This simple farmer's soup combines the heartiness of vegetables and sausages with the creamy richness of milk, making it a comforting dish.


## 15 .CREAMY PRAWN AND PEA SOUP

**Preparation and cooking time 45 minutes**

**Level : Medium hard**

This is a Prawn and Green Pea Soup with a creamy white sauce base, using small frozen prawns, green peas, milk, and a flour-thickened white sauce.

**Ingredients:**

- 1 cup small frozen prawns, thawed

- 1 cup green peas ( canned or frozen)

- 2 cups milk or reconstituted milk or coconut milk

- 1 tablespoon flour

- 1 tablespoon butter

- 1 small onion, chopped

- 2 cloves garlic, minced or 1/2 teaspoon of it's powder

- 1 cup vegetable or chicken broth

- Salt and pepper, to taste

- A pinch of cinnamon (optional)

- Fresh parsley or cilantro chopped or a pinch of dried herbs

**Method :**

1. Prepare the white sauce in a medium saucepan, by melting the butter over low heat. Add the flour and whisk continuously to form a smooth paste (roux). Cook for 1-2 minutes on low heat to remove the raw flour taste, but don't let it brown.

2. Gradually pour in the milk while whisking to prevent lumps. Continue stirring until the mixture thickens into a smooth white sauce. Turn off heat . Set aside.

3. Cook the base by heating oil or butter in another pot, sauté the chopped onions and garlic until softened and fragrant.

4. Stir in the green peas and thawed prawns. Cook for 5 minutes, until the prawns turn pink and the peas are heated through

5. Pour in the broth and bring the mixture to a simmer. Cook for 10 minutes more on low heat .Then, gradually stir in the white sauce until the soup is smooth and creamy.

6. Season with salt, pepper, and a pinch of cinnamon , if desired. Rest the soup for 5 minutes, allowing the flavors to combine

7. Ladle the soup into bowls, garnish with fresh or dried herbs and serve hot.

This light yet creamy prawn and pea soup is perfect for a quick meal, for seafood lovers with a delicate seafood flavor balanced by the richness of the white sauce.

Note : A teaspoon of grated Parmesan cheese may be added for extra flavor ( optional )

# CHAPTER FOUR

**LUNCH DISHES**

**1.SEAFOOD RICE**
Preparation and cooking time 50 min
Level : Medium hard
Ingredients:
- 300g medium shrimp, peeled and deveined
- 300g mussels or clams cleaned or obtained frozen
- one crab , cleaned or small canned crabmeat ( optional )
- 300g squid, cut into rings or obtained frozen
- 1 large onion, chopped
- 4 garlic cloves, minced or a level teaspoon of garlic powder
- 2 ripe tomatoes, chopped

- 1 bell pepper, chopped

- 1 tablespoon olive oil or butter

- 3 cups fish stock or substitute by dissolving 1 tablespoon of fish sauce in 3 cups of water
- 1.5 cup basmati rice
- 2 sprigs of fresh cilantro, chopped or a pinch of dried herbs
- Salt and pepper to taste
Method :

1.  Wash and soak the rice for ten minutes. Drain. Heat the oil or butter in a round casserole and sauté the onions until translucent.

1.  Add the garlic , sauté ten seconds and then add chopped tomatoes and , pepper and the cilantro or a pinch of dried herbs . Sauté five minutes .

2. Add the cleaned fresh or frozen shrimps , the fresh or frozen clams , the fresh or frozen squid and the shelled crab ( if using ) . Add two cups of water . Salt and pepper to taste . Bring to the boil and cook the seafood around twenty minutes in low heat until all water is absorbed .

3. Add the three cups of fish stock water . Bring to the boil . Lower the heat and add the drained rice and salt to taste . Cook until the rice has absorbed all the water . This takes around 12-15 minutes .

4. Serve hot with the simple onion and tomato salad . (The recipe for that is in the salad section) . This is a main dish in itself .

## 2. RICE WITH FISH KEDGEREE

Preparation and cooking time 45 minutes

Level : Medium hard

Ingredients:

- 1 cup basmati rice, washed and soaked for 15 minutes

- 250g boneless fish fillet chunks (any white boneless chunky fish)

- 1 medium onion, chopped

- 1-2 green chilies, slit deseeded ( optional )

- 1 teaspoon turmeric powder

- 2 bay leaves ( optional )

- 1 tablespoon tomato paste or sauce

- 2 hard-boiled eggs, cut into halves or quarters

- 1-inch piece of ginger, finely chopped or 1/2 teaspoon of its powder

- 2 cloves of garlic, finely chopped or 1/2 teaspoon of its powder

- 1 teaspoon garam masala powder

- 2 sprigs fresh cilantro or parsley leaves, or a pinch of dried herbs

- Salt and pepper to taste

- 2 tablespoons ghee , butter or oil

- 3 cups water or fish stock ( Add a tablespoon of fish sauce to 3 cups warm water or 1 store bought stock cube

- Lemon wedges for serving

- Few fried raisins or sultanas or roasted slivered almonds
or 1 teaspoon of grated Parmesan cheese ( optional )

Method:

1. Poach the fish fillets in a non stick pan or saucepan ( approximately 4 chunks ) in one cup salted water or fish stock with pepper and half of the turmeric and garam masala , for about 10 minutes, until they are cooked and still stays firm Remove, drain, reserve stock and Set aside.

2. In a separate pan, sauté the onions in oil or ghee or butter and when they are translucent add the ginger and garlic , remaining turmeric , tomato paste or sauce and garam masala . Adjust salt and pepper .

3. Add the basmati rice and water (use the reserved stock from the fish for extra flavor) . The total water including stock should not exceed two cups . Add the bay leaves if using and add the cilantro or parsley or the pinch of dried herbs .

4. Cook on low heat about 12-14 minutes until the rice has absorbed all the water and is cooked and tender . Turn off the heat . Rest ten minutes and stir the rice gently mixing the flavors

5. Add the fish chunks to the pan and gently fold in , ensuring the fish does not break and is coated with the spicy rice mixture .

6. Adjust the seasoning, and add more salt, pepper, or lemon juice as needed. Garnish with fresh cilantro or parsley leaves or a pinch of dried herbs and boiled sliced or quartered eggs. If using raisins or grated Parmesan cheese , add it now . ( optional )

7. Garnish with lemon slices if needed and serve hot with plain yoghurt and sliced cucumber ( optional )

This Anglo-Indian kedgeree is perfect for lunch, bringing out the fusion of British and Indian culinary influences.

## 3. FUSION BIRIYANI ANGLO INDIAN STYLE

Preparation and cooking time 45 minutes

Level : Medium hard

Ingredients :

- 6 medium chicken drumsticks or thighs
- 1 cup basmati rice
- 1 tablespoon level garam masala
- 1 tablespoon tomato paste or sauce
- 3 tablespoon butter or oil or ghee
- 1 teaspoon level turmeric powder
- 1/2 teaspoon cinnamon powder

- 4 cloves whole

- 3 boiled eggs , ( for serving )

- 1 cup yoghurt
- 4 sprigs cilantro or parsley chopped or 2 pinch of dried herbs

- Salt and pepper to taste

Method :

1. Steam the rice in rice cooker or manually with 2 cups of water , one tablespoon oil or butter or ghee and salt to taste , for 12-14 minutes on low heat until all water is absorbed and the rice is cooked . Keep a watch not to burn it if cooking manually . Set aside

2. In a pot heat the remaining oil or butter or ghee and sauté the onions , cloves , with a pinch of the herbs or 2 sprigs of cilantro until translucent . Add garam masala , cinnamon, turmeric , tomato paste or sauce , salt and pepper to taste . Sauté one minute and add half the yoghurt and 1.5 cups warm water .

3. Cook the chicken on low heat covered , until it's done and all the water is absorbed . Do not burn the sauce. The chicken should be without any visible gravy but should be moist . Turn off the heat
.

4. Add the steamed or cooked rice to the cooked chicken . Add remaining chopped cilantro or a pinch of the herbs . Toss well without breaking the chicken . The dish should not have liquid . Garnish with the boiled eggs for each serving .

5. Skin and Chop the cucumber .Combine with the remaining yoghurt in a small bowl. Season with salt as pepper .

6. Serve this fusion Biriyani , with the yoghurt cucumber sauce or pickles

CHAPTER FIVE

PAN ROASTS , GRILLS

1. PIRI PIRI CHICKEN

Preparation and Cooking time 1 hour for marinade ,35 min for cooking

Level : Medium hard

Ingredients:

- 4 chicken thighs or medium large drumsticks

- 2 tablespoons Piri Piri sauce (store-bought ) or substitute by combining 1 tablespoon of tomato sauce and one tablespoon of either ketchup or mild hot sauce

- 1 tablespoon lemon juice

- 1 tablespoon olive oil

- 1 teaspoon minced garlic or 1/2 level teaspoon of garlic powder

- 1 /2 level teaspoon paprika

- 1 /2 level teaspoon curry powder

- Salt and pepper to taste

- Fresh cilantro or parsley leaves or a pinch of dried herbs for garnish

Method :

1.  Marinate the Chicken: - In a large bowl, mix the Piri Piri or tomato sauce, lemon juice, olive oil, minced garlic, paprika, curry powder , pepper, salt, and pepper.

- Add the chicken thighs or drumsticks to the marinade, ensuring they are well-coated.

- Cover the bowl and let the chicken marinate for at least 1 hour, it can be also marinated overnight, in the refrigerator if that's more convenient.

2. Preheat : Preheat your oven to 200 degrees C or set up your air fryer 180 degrees C for medium-high heat.

- If using an oven, place the marinated chicken on a baking tray lined with aluminum foil or parchment paper.

- If air fryer is used , grill the chicken on air frying disposable liner ( available in stores especially for the air fryer ) , to prevent sticking.

3. Cook the Chicken: - If using Oven : Roast the chicken for 25-30 minutes, turning halfway through, until the chicken is cooked through and has a crispy, slightly charred exterior.

- If using Air fryer Grill: Grill the chicken for 25-30 minutes, turning once to ensure even cooking without charring.

4. Rest and Garnish: - Once the chicken is cooked, remove it from the oven or air fryer grill and let it rest for 5 minutes.

- Garnish with fresh cilantro leaves ( optional ) before serving.

Serving Suggestions: - Serve the Piri Piri chicken with a side of roasted vegetables ( optional ) , steamed rice, flatbread , warm bun or hot rolls . A cooling plain yogurt dip also pairs well with the spiciness of the chicken.

## 2. PAN ROASTED / FRIED MUSSELS

Preparation and cooking time 1 hour

Level : Hard

Ingredients:

- 500g fresh mussels (cleaned and inedible parts removed )
- 2 tablespoon oil (olive oil , coconut oil or vegetable oil)
- 1 onion, finely chopped
- 2 garlic cloves, minced or 1/2 teaspoon of its powder
- 1-inch ginger, grated or 1/2 teaspoon of its powder
- 2 green chilies, chopped deseeded (optional)
- 1 teaspoon turmeric powder
- 1 teaspoon paprika or chili powder (adjust to taste)
- 1 teaspoon black pepper powder

- 1 teaspoon garam masala

- 1 tablespoon lemon juice

- 2 tablespoons tomato paste , hot sauce or tomato sauce

- Salt to taste

- Fresh cilantro or parsley leaves or a pinch of dried herbs for garnish

Method :

1. Clean the mussels thoroughly by scrubbing the shells and removing the beard (fibrous strand). Discard any mussels that are open and don't close when tapped. They may be contaminated

2. Boil the mussels in salted water for about 20 minutes until they open. Drain and discard any mussels that still remain closed. Set aside.

1. Heat oil in a pan or skillet over medium heat.

2. Add the chopped onions and sauté until golden brown.

3. Stir in the minced garlic, or its powder , grated ginger, or its powder and chopped green chilies if using . Sauté for 2-3 minutes until fragrant.

4. Add the turmeric powder, paprika or chili powder, tomato paste or sauce and pepper . Cook the spices for another 2 minutes.

5. Add the boiled mussels meat to the pan, stirring well to coat them in the spice mixture.

6. Cook for another 15 minutes on medium heat , with 1/4 cup of water , covered until it's well cooked, turning the mussels occasionally to ensure they are well-seasoned . Turn off the heat when slightly crisp on the outside. Test one to see if easily chewable. If not , add few tablespoons of water and cook further 5 min on low heat

7. Sprinkle garam masala and drizzle lemon juice over the mussels.

8. Stir for another minute, turn off the heat. Let it rest ten minutes covered

9. Garnish with fresh cilantro or parsley leaves or a pinch of dried herbs

Serve these Anglo-Indian Pan-Fried Mussels as a snack or side dish, with bread, steamed or cooked rice, flatbread , or on their own with a slice of lemon for a delicious and spicy seafood treat!


## 3. CHICKEN LIVER PAN FRIED

Preparation and cooking time 45 minutes

Level : Easy

Ingredients:

- 500 grams chicken liver, cleaned

- 2 large onions, sliced
- 2 green chilies, slit (optional, adjust to taste)
- 2 tablespoons ginger-garlic paste or 1/2 teaspoon each of their powders
- 2 teaspoons tomato paste or tomato sauce or ketchup
- 1 teaspoon curry powder
- 1/2 teaspoon turmeric powder
- 1 teaspoon paprika or red chili powder
- 1/2 teaspoon garam masala
- 1/4 teaspoon black pepper
- Fresh cilantro or parsley leaves or a pinch of dried herbs for garnish
- Salt to taste
- Oil for frying

Method:

1. Clean and boil the chicken liver with salt in one cup of water until cooked . Reserve the stock . Drain and cut the into bite-sized small pieces. Pat dry with paper towels to remove excess moisture.

2.Heat oil in a pan over medium-high heat. Add the chicken liver pieces lower the heat and fry until they are golden brown and cooked through, about 10 minutes. Remove and set aside.

3. In the same pan, add a bit more oil if needed. Add the sliced onions and green chilies (if using). Cook until the onions are caramelized and golden brown.

4. Stir in the ginger-garlic paste or their powders and cook until aromatic , for a minute .

5. Add curry powder, turmeric powder, paprika or red chili powder, tomato paste or sauce pepper and salt. Cook for a couple of minutes until the spices are well-blended and aromatic.

6. Return the fried chicken liver to the pan. Mix well to coat with the spice mixture. Drizzle 2 tablespoons of stock if it's too dry . Cook for another 5 minutes, stirring occasionally, until everything is well combined and the liver pieces are well-coated with the spices.

7. Add Garam Masala: Stir in the garam masala and black pepper. Cook for another 2 minutes.

8. Garnish and Serve: Garnish with fresh cilantro or parsley leaves or the pinch of dried herbs and serve hot with steamed or cooked rice , lightly toasted bread or any flatbread like naan .

This recipe provides a flavorful and spicy chicken liver dish that's typically prepared every week in Anglo-Indian households.

## 4. PAN FRIED ( HOT ) SHEEP OR BEEF LIVER

Preparation and cooking time 45 minutes

Level : Medium hard

Ingredients:

- 500 grams beef or lamb liver, cleaned and cut into chunks

- 2 large onions, finely sliced

- 2 tomatoes, chopped or 2 tablespoons of tomato paste or sauce

- 2 tablespoons ginger-garlic paste or 1/2 teaspoon each of their powders

- 1 teaspoon curry powder

- 1/2 teaspoon turmeric powder

- 1 teaspoon paprika or red chili powder

- 1/2 teaspoon garam masala

- 1/4 teaspoon black pepper

- Fresh cilantro or parsley leaves or a pinch of dried herbs for garnish

- Salt to taste

- Oil for pan frying

Method:

1. Clean the liver pieces thoroughly, removing any membranes and excess fat. Boil the chunks in salted water for 20 minutes or until cooked through . Slice into bite sized pieces when cool and set aside. Reserve stock .

2. Heat oil in a pan over medium heat . Add sliced onions and cook until golden brown. Stir in ginger-garlic paste or their powders and cook until fragrant.

3. Add chopped tomatoes, or the tomato sauce , curry powder, turmeric powder, paprika or red chili powder, and salt. Cook until the tomatoes soften or the sauce is cooked and the oil starts to separate.

4. Add the liver pieces to the pan. Stir well to coat with the spice mixture. Add two tablespoons of the stock and cook on low heat , stir frying , until the liver is cooked through and has absorbed the spices, about 10 minutes.

5. Add garam masala and black pepper. Stir fry for another 2-3 minutes.

6. Garnish with fresh cilantro or parsley leaves or a pinch of dried herbs and serve hot with steamed or cooked rice , flatbread , hot rolls or warm bread.

## 5. PAN FRIED POTTI ( BOVINE INTESTINES )

Preparation and cooking time 1 hour

Level : Hard

Ingredients:

For cleansing:

- 500g bovine intestines (cleaned thoroughly)
- 2 tbsp salt
- 2 tbsp vinegar or lemon juice

For the Roast :

- 2 tablespoons oil
- 1 large onion, finely chopped
- 2 garlic cloves, minced or 1/2 teaspoon of its powder
- 1-inch ginger, grated or 1/2 teaspoon of its powder
- 2 green chilies, slit deseeded ( optional )
- 2 tomatoes, finely chopped or 2 tablespoons of tomato paste or thick tomato sauce
- 1 teaspoon turmeric powder
- 1 teaspoon paprika or red chili powder
- 1 teaspoon pepper powder
- 1 teaspoon curry powder
- 1 tsp garam masala
- Salt to taste
- 1 sprig cilantro or parsley leaves or a pinch of dried herbs
- 2 tablespoons vinegar or lemon juice
- Fresh cilantro or parsley leaves or a pinch of dried herbs for garnish

Method :

1. Thoroughly clean the intestines by washing them multiple times under running water.

2. Rub the intestines with salt and vinegar (or lemon juice), then rinse them again to remove any residual smell or impurities.

3. Boil the cleaned intestines in water for 30 minutes to further clean and tenderize them. Drain the water and set the intestines aside to cool.

4. Heat oil in a deep pan or wok

5. Add the chopped onions and cook until golden brown.

6. Stir in the garlic, ginger, and green chilies, if using , and sauté for 2-3 minutes until fragrant.

7. Add the chopped tomatoes or the tomato sauce and cook until they soften and blend into the mixture.

8. Add turmeric powder, chili or paprika powder, pepper powder, and curry powder. Cook the spices for 3-4 minutes until the raw smell disappears.

9. Cut the boiled intestines into bite-sized pieces and add them to the pan. Stir well to coat the intestines with the spice mixture.

10. Add vinegar or lemon juice , and season with salt. Add half cup of water .Cook on low heat for 10-15 minutes, stir frying on medium heat until the intestines are well-roasted , or just becoming roasted and dry , and the spices have absorbed into the meat.

11. . Sprinkle garam masala on top and give it a final stir.

12. Garnish with fresh cilantro leaves or a pinch of dried herbs . The dish should be moist and without visible fluid

Serve this Anglo-Indian Roast Potti with roasted vegetables or mashed potato ( optional ) steamed or cooked rice, toasted bread, flatbread or buns . The slow roasting enhances the flavors, making it a savory and spicy and hearty dish with a unique texture.

Anglo-Indian Roast Potti, a dish made from bovine intestines is a delicacy that's included in the menu at least once a month in Anglo Indian households , and even for celebrations and feasts , being a dish that is roasted to perfection, with rich flavors and textures that are unique to Anglo-Indian cuisine .

# 6 . SPICY PAN ROASTED BOVINE UDDER

Preparation and cooking time 1 hour

Level : Somewhat hard

Ingredients:

- 500 grams cow udder, cleaned well and cut into chunks

- 2 large onions, finely sliced

- 2 tomatoes, chopped or two tablespoons of tomato paste

- 2 tablespoons ginger-garlic paste or1/2 teaspoon each of their powder

- 1 teaspoon curry powder

- 1/2 teaspoon turmeric powder

- 1 teaspoon paprika ( optional )

- 1/2 teaspoon garam masala

- 1/2 teaspoon black pepper

- 1 tablespoon lemon juice or vinegar

- Fresh cilantro or parsley leaves for garnish

- Salt to taste

- Oil for frying

Method:

1. Clean the cow udder thoroughly, removing any membranes and excess fat. Cut into large chunks . Boil in water with a little salt for about 30 minutes until tender. Make sure it's cooked through . Drain and set aside . Reserve stock

2. Heat oil in a large non stick pan over medium heat. Slice the cooked udder into bite sized pieces. Add the udder pieces and stir fry on low heat until they are golden brown and crisp. Remove and set aside.

3. In the same pan, add more oil if needed. Add sliced onions and cook until they are caramelized and golden brown.

4. Stir in ginger-garlic paste or their powders and cook for a minute until fragrant. Add chopped tomatoes, curry powder, turmeric powder, paprika if using , black pepper, and salt. Cook

until the tomatoes soften and the oil separates from the sauce or mixture.

5.Add the fried udder pieces back into the pan. Lower the heat . Stir well to coat the pieces with the spice mixture. Add two tablespoons of stock and sauté for about 5 minutes to allow the flavors to combine

6.Stir in garam masala and lemon juice or vinegar. Sauté for another 5 minutes. The dish should not have visible fluid but should be moist .

7. Garnish with fresh cilantro or parsley leaves or a pinch of dried herbs and serve hot with steamed or cooked rice , warm rolls , flatbread like naan or lightly toasted bread .

This dish is rich in flavor , it's an acquired taste and makes for a hearty, flavorful meal.

## 6. SQUID : SPICY PAN FRY ( KALAMARI )
Preparation and cooking time 45 minutes
Level : Medium hard
Ingredients :
250g Frozen Squid
1 small Bell pepper
1 firm tomato or 2 tablespoons of tomato paste or sauce
1 onion
1/2 teaspoon garlic powder
A pinch of dried herbs
1 tablespoon lemon juice
1 teaspoon garam masala
1 level teaspoon pepper powder
1 tablespoon oil
Method :

1. Thaw the frozen squid and cook it in 1 cup of lightly salted water for about 20 minutes or until cooked well . If using fresh squid , clean well and cook for 30 minutes . Drain and set aside . Reserve stock .

1. Sauté the onions in the oil until golden brown. Toss in the sliced bell pepper . Cook for five minutes . Add the sliced firm tomato or the tomato paste and sauté for five minutes.

2. Add the garlic powder garam masala and pepper . After a minute add the cooked drained squid with three tablespoons of the stock . Lower the heat and stir fry until all moisture is absorbed and lightly browned

3. Add the lemon juice and the pinch of herbs and toss well . Turn off the heat . Rest the squid 5 minutes and serve with roasted vegetables ( optional ) , flatbread , pita bread , steamed or cooked rice .

## 7. PAN FRIED OKRA

Preparation and cooking time 30 minutes
Level : Somewhat easy
Ingredients:

- 250 okra washed and dried

- 2 tablespoons rice flour
- 2 tablespoons chicken pea flour (gram flour)
- 1 teaspoon paprika or red chili powder
- 1/2 teaspoon turmeric powder
- 1/2 teaspoon garam masala
- Salt to taste

- Oil for frying

Method:

1.Trim the tops and tails of the ladies' fingers and cut them crosswise into thin slices. Ensure they are completely dry to avoid spluttering when frying.

2. In a bowl, combine rice flour, gram flour , paprika or red chili powder, turmeric powder, garam masala, and salt.

3. Add the sliced okra to the spice mixture and toss until the pieces are evenly coated with the flour and spices.

4.Heat oil in a frying pan over medium heat. You need just enough oil to shallow fry the okra.

5. Once the oil is hot, add the coated okra slices in batches, ensuring not to overcrowd the pan. Stir fry on medium until the okra is crispy and golden brown, about 10 minutes . Ensure it does not burn as it contains no liquid .

6.Remove the fried okra with a slotted spoon and drain on paper towels to remove excess oil.

7. Garnish with a squeeze of lemon juice if desired.

Serve the fried ladies' finger hot as a side dish with steamed or cooked rice or flatbread .


## 8 . GRILLED BEEF SKEWERS

Preparation and cooking time 45 minutes

Level : Medium hard


Ingredients:

- 500g minced beef
- 1 small onion, finely chopped
- 2 garlic cloves, minced or 1/2 teaspoon of its powder
- 1 teaspoon paprika

- 1 tablespoon tomato paste or tomato sauce

- 1 tablespoon fresh parsley, chopped or a pinch of dried herbs
- Salt and pepper to taste
- 1 tablespoon olive oil
- Wooden or metal skewers

Method :

1. Prepare the Skewers . If using wooden skewers, soak them in water for about 20-30 minutes to prevent them from burning during cooking.

2. In a large mixing bowl, combine the minced beef, onion, garlic, paprika or chili powder, tomato paste or sauce parsley or dried herbs , salt, and pepper. Mix well until all ingredients are evenly distributed.

3.Take a small portion of the beef mixture and shape it around the skewer, pressing gently to ensure the meat sticks. You can make them cylindrical or slightly flattened.

4. Place the skewers in the refrigerator for about 30 minutes to firm up.

5. Preheat your grill or air fryer to medium-high heat. 180 degrees C . Brush the beef with olive oil and grill for 7minutes ( on each side) , or until fully cooked. If using air fryer use smaller length skewers to fit and use the air fryer liner to place them.

6. Or Pan Fry . Heat some olive oil in a pan over medium-high heat. Cook the skewered beef for 7 minutes (on each side ) until browned and cooked through.

Serve the Beef skewers hot with a side of tomato salad .

( Recipe in salad section )

Alternatively , serve with grilled potato wedges or roasted vegetables ( optional)

## 9. SIMPLE PAN FRIED SAUSAGES

Preparation and cooking time 30 minutes

Level : Easy

Ingredients :

- 250g beef or pork sausages

- 2 tablespoons tomato paste or tomato sauce

- 1 chopped onion

- 1 boiled potato ( optional )

- 2 cloves garlic or 1/2 teaspoon of its powder

- A pinch of dried herbs ( optional )

- 1 tablespoon of oil

- 1 teaspoon of garam masala ( optional )

- 1 level teaspoon of pepper

- Salt to taste .

Method :

1. Boil the sausages in water for about 10-15 minutes until it's cooked through . Cool and slice into 1 cm pieces .

1. Heat oil and sauté the chopped onion until translucent . Add the garlic or its powder and cook for a minute .

2. Add the salt and pepper , chopped cilantro or dried herbs , tomato paste or sauce , garam masala if using , and the sliced sausages . Sauté for five minutes on low heat until sausages start to brown slightly .

3. Add the chopped boiled potato if using , and lemon juice and toss until well mixed . Turn off the heat and allow to rest covered for 5 minutes . and serve on its own or with flatbread , pita bred , bun or warm rolls .

Note : For those who like a cheesy flavor , sprinkle a teaspoon of grated Parmesan cheese ( optional)

## 10. GRILLED ( OR AIR FRIED ) WHOLE CHICKEN LEGS

Preparation and cooking time 1 hour

Level : Medium hard

Ingredients :

- 4 Chicken whole legs with skin
- 2 tablespoon all purpose flour
- 1 teaspoon black pepper
- 1 teaspoon paprika or red chilly powder
- 2 tablespoons oil
- 1 egg beaten
- Salt to taste

Method :

1. Place the whole chicken legs in a bowl and sprinkle salt and half the pepper with the paprika . Toss well . Keep aside for ten minutes .

1. Pre heat the oven or the air fryer at 180 degrees C
2. Beat the egg . Add the remaining pepper to the flour and a pinch of salt .
3. Coat the whole chicken legs in the beaten egg and roll them on the flour and lay them on a baking tray lined with lightly greased foil or air fryer on parchment paper that fits to its size
4. Drizzle the 2 tablespoons of oil on all the pieces .
5. Bake or grill for 30-35 minutes until crisp and cooked depending on the size and the grill or air fryer . Turn once

half way through, with wooden tongs . If using air fryer , grill two at a time .

Serve on its own or with mashed potato , salad or steamed vegetables ( optional ) , or flatbread , warm buns , rolls or just a yoghurt dip .

## 11. GRILLED MUTTON KEEMA BALLS

Preparation and cooking time 35 minutes
Level : Medium hard
Ingredients :

- 500g Mutton or Lamb mince
- 1 chopped onion
- 1 level teaspoon black pepper
- 1 teaspoon of tomato sauce or paste
- 1 teaspoon curry powder ( optional )
- 1/2 a teaspoon cinnamon powder ( optional )
- A pinch of dried herbs
- 1 tablespoon lemon juice
- 1 egg ( needed only if the mince does not shape )
- Salt to taste

Method :

1. Preheat the oven or air fryer to 175 degrees C.
2. Add chopped onions , pepper , salt to taste , herbs , cinnamon powder , if using ; to the minced lamb and shape into lime sized balls . If it does not shape , add the whole egg and combine to enable the shape .
3. Place on parchment paper on the grill rack in the oven or

on the air fryer liner and grill for 20 minutes or until done . Keep a watch on it as oven temperatures may vary . It should have a good grilled color .

4. Serve on its own or with ketchup or a simple tomato salad .

## 12. SIMPLE GRILLED FISH

Preparation and cooking time 40 minutes

Level : Medium hard

500g chunks of fish , preferably boneless . Or one large boneless fillet

1 tablespoon tomato paste or sauce

1 teaspoon black pepper powder

1 tablespoon lemon juice

Salt to taste

Method :

1. Preheat the oven or air fryer to 175 degrees C

1. Combine the tomato paste or sauce with black pepper and salt to taste
2. Score the fish fillets or chunks lightly . One score per chunk or three scores if using a large fillet .
3. Smear the seasoned tomato paste all over with a spoon
4. Grill or air fry on parchment paper or air fry liners for 20 minutes or so until done . Do not flip , but make sure the fish is cooked and grilled well . Add extra time if it's not done . Depends on the oven temperature.
5. Serve with simple tomato salad or tomato sauce or with a yoghurt dip and cucumber ( optional )

## 13. PAN FRIED RICE

Preparation and cooking time 45 min
Level : Medium hard
- 1 cup basmati rice or any long grain rice steamed , or cooked
- 1 cup cooked sliced sausages ( chicken , or beef or pork sausage )
- 1 cup steamed vegetables ( either frozen broccoli and frozen peas , or steamed carrots and frozen cut beans )

- 2 tablespoons butter or ghee or oil

- 1 chopped onion

- 2 cloves chopped garlic or 1/2 teaspoon of its powder

- 1 teaspoon level black pepper powder

- 1 tablespoon tomato paste or sauce or ketchup

- 1 tablespoons lemon juice

- 1 teaspoon sugar

- 2 sprigs of cilantro or parsley or 1 pinch of dried herbs

Method :

1. Wash and soak the rice for ten minutes . Cook the rice with two cups of water on low heat . Around 12-14 minutes for basmati rice . Alternatively cook the rice in a rice cooker until done .

1. In a large non stick pan heat the butter or ghee or oil in medium heat. Sauté the onions with the garlic until lightly browned .

2. Add sliced sausages sugar , tomato paste , black pepper and salt to taste . Sauté five minute until sausages start to brown .

3. Add the steamed vegetables. Sauté for five minutes until the vegetable are almost fried.
4. Add rice and lemon juice and the herbs . Toss to coat well . Lower the heat and pan fry the cooked rice with the vegetables for ten minutes without burning . Add more butter or ghee or oil , if required .
5. Turn off the heat and rest it for five minutes covered.
6. Pan fried rice should not have moisture .
7. Serve each serving with a fried egg on top ( optional )

This is a filling dish and a comfort food .


## 14. DEEP FRIED CAULIFLOWER AND POTATO
Preparation and cooking time 45 minutes
Level : Medium hard
Ingredients:

- Half a small cauliflower broken into florets
- 2 medium potatoes washed cut into wedges with skin
- 1 tablespoon tomato paste or tomato sauce
- Salt and pepper to taste
- Oil 1 inch deep for frying

Method :

1. Wash and scrub the potatoes well . Cut each into eight wedges with the skins .

1. Divide the cauliflower into florets . Remove unwanted parts and stems . Retain only a small bit of its stem close to the florets .

2.  In a bowl combine half a tablespoon of the tomato paste or sauce with the wedges . Season with salt and pepper .

3.  Another bowl combine the cauliflower florets with remaining tomato paste or sauce . Season with salt and pepper .

4.  Heat the oil and fry the potato wedges eight at a time . Fry until golden brown and crisp on the outside . Remove with a slotted spoon . Drain on paper towel . Fry the other batch of wedges . Drain on paper towel. Alternatively use the air fryer with its liner with a drizzle of oil and air fry for 25 minutes on 180 degrees C , or until done

5.  Fry the cauliflower in the same oil in one batch . Stirring every two minutes until evenly fried and a good golden brown color . Do not burn . Remove with slotted spoon . Drain on paper towel . Alternatively, use the air fryer liner and 2 tablespoons of oil and air fry for 20 min on 175 degrees C , or until done

6.  Serve together with warm buns and ketchup ( optional )

7.  This is a comfort food .

## CHAPTER SIX

## CURRIES

## 1. PUMPKIN CURRY ( FUSION DISH )
Preparation and cooking time 30 min
Level : Easy
Ingredients:
- 500 grams pumpkin, peeled and cut into cubes
- 1 large onion, finely chopped
- 2 tomatoes, chopped
- 2 cloves garlic, minced or 1/2 teaspoon of garlic powder
- 1 teaspoon ginger or 1/2 teaspoon of ginger powder
- 1 teaspoon turmeric powder
- 1 teaspoon paprika
- 1 teaspoon curry powder
- 1/2 teaspoon garam masala
- 1/2 cup milk or reconstituted milk or coconut milk
- A few sprigs cilantro or parsley leaves chopped or a pinch of dried herbs for garnish
- Salt to taste
- Oil or butter
Method:
1. Heat oil in a pan and sauté the aromatics . Add chopped onions and cook until golden brown. Add garlic and ginger and garlic , cooking until fragrant.

2. Stir in chopped tomatoes, turmeric powder, paprika powder, curry powder, and salt. Cook until the tomatoes are soft and the oil separates from the mixture.

3. Add the pumpkin cubes and stir to coat with the spices. Pour in a little water to help the pumpkin cook. Cover and simmer on medium heat until the pumpkin is tender, about 20 minutes.

4. Stir in milk or coconut milk and garam masala. Cook for a few more minutes until the curry thickens and is well blended.

5. Garnish and Serve: Garnish with fresh cilantro or parsley leaves or a pinch of dried herbs and serve with steamed rice or toast , bun or flatbread.

Note : Sprinkle a tablespoon of grated Parmesan or cheddar cheese for a cheesy flavor ( optional )

# 2. CRAB CURRY

Preparation and cooking time 45 minutes

Level : Medium hard

Ingredients:

- 500 grams crab (cleaned and cut into pieces) or two small cans of crab meat .

- 2 large onions, finely chopped

- 2 tomatoes, chopped

- 2 tablespoons ginger-garlic paste or half a teaspoon each of ginger and garlic powder

- 1/2 cup desiccated coconut, ( optional ) or substitute with 1 cup milk or reconstituted milk or coconut milk

- 1 teaspoon turmeric powder

- 1 teaspoon paprika or red chili powder

- 1 teaspoon curry powder

- 1 teaspoon garam masala

- 1 bay leaf ( optional )

- 2 green chilies, slit deseeded (optional)

- Fresh cilantro or parsley leaves or a pinch of dried herbs for garnish

- Salt to taste

- Oil

Method:

1.  Grind grated coconut if using with a little water to make a smooth paste. Otherwise substitute with one cup of milk or coconut milk . Set aside

2. Heat oil in a large pan, add bay leaf if using . Once they sizzle, add chopped onions and sauté until golden brown. Add ginger-garlic paste or powder and cook for a minute only .

3. Add chopped tomatoes, turmeric powder, paprika or red chili powder, curry powder, and salt. Cook until the tomatoes are softened and the oil begins to separate from the mixture.

4. Stir in the crab pieces and coconut paste or milk . Cook for a few minutes, then add a cup of water. Bring to a boil, then reduce the heat and simmer until the crab is cooked through, about 20 minutes.

5. Finish with Garam Masala and cook for another 5 minutes.

6. Garnish with fresh cilantro or parsley leaves or a pinch of dried herbs and serve hot with a light salad or steamed rice , flat bread or lightly toasted bread

## 3. MINCED BEEF BALL CURRY :

Preparation and cooking time 40 minutes

Level : Easy

- Ingredients:

- 500 g Minced beef
- 2 medium onions
- green chilies or a quarter of a bell pepper ( optional ),
- ginger-garlic paste, or half a teaspoon each of ginger and garlic powder
- 1/2 a teaspoon of turmeric,
- 1/2 a teaspoon of garam masala,
- 1 level teaspoon Curry powder,
- A pinch of cinnamon powder
- 4 whole cloves ( optional)
- 2 tomatoes

- A small cup of store bought coconut milk or milk or reconstituted milk
- 1 small cup of warm water
- Pepper and salt to taste
- A tablespoon of butter or oil

- Method:

1. Chop both the onions or slice them . Mix the minced beef with half of the chopped onions, green chilies or chopped bell pepper , if using , half of the ginger-garlic paste or powder , turmeric, garam masala, and salt. Form into small balls size of limes .

2. Heat oil or butter in a non stick pan and fry the beef balls in shall oil until lightly browned. Remove and Set aside.

3. In the same pan, sauté remaining chopped onions, remaining ginger-garlic paste or their powders , and tomatoes until soft.

4. Add turmeric, curry powder, cinnamon , and cloves if using , cooking until the spices are aromatic.

5. Pour in the cup of milk or coconut milk plus one cup of water and let it simmer on medium heat , then add the fried beef balls and cook until tender , until sauce is thick and mince is fully cooked. Around 20 minutes

6. Serve hot with roasted or steamed vegetables or mashed potato ( optional ) , steamed rice , bun , flatbread or lightly warmed bread.

## 4. TROTTERS CURRY ( PAYA )

Preparation and cooking time : 2-3 hours , slow cooking , depends on trotter . Note : It's best to get the trotter sliced at time of purchase from the store or butcher . If not they may not fit in the pot .

Level : Medium hard
- Ingredients:
- 2 Trotters (goat or lamb)
- 2 medium onions
- 2 tomatoes
- 1 teaspoon ginger-garlic paste, or 1/2 a teaspoon each of their powder
- 1/2 teaspoon turmeric
- 1 level teaspoon paprika
- 1/2 teaspoon Curry powder ( optional )
- 1/2 teaspoon garam masala
- 1 small stick cinnamon, or 1/2 teaspoons of it's powder
- 4 cloves
- A cup of milk or reconstituted milk or coconut milk
- 2 bay leaves ( optional)
- a sprig of cilantro or parsley leaves, or a pinch of dried herbs
- Salt and pepper to taste

- 2 tablespoon of oil or butter

- Method:
1. Clean the trotters thoroughly and set aside.
2. In a large pot, heat oil or butter and sauté bay leaves, if using , cinnamon, and cloves, until fragrant.
3. Add finely chopped onions and cook until golden brown, then add ginger-garlic paste or its powder and cook for a half minute
4. Stir in chopped tomatoes, turmeric, paprika , curry powder, if using , and salt, cooking until the tomatoes soften and the oil separates.
5. Add the trotters and water, then cover and simmer until the trotters are tender and the curry thickens. This might take a couple of hours or more depending on the toughness of the trotters.

6. Add garam masala and cook for a few more minutes. Turn off the heat and add the cup of milk

7. Garnish with chopped cilantro or parsley or the pinch of herbs . Serve hot with steamed or roasted vegetables , mashed potato ( optional ) , steamed or cooked rice, flatbread , bun or lightly toasted bread.


## 5 .RAILWAY MUTTON CURRY

Preparation and cooking time :

Marinate 1 hour . Cooking 45 minutes

Level : Medium hard

Ingredients:

- 1 kg mutton (cut into pieces)

- 2 large onions (finely sliced)

- 2 tomatoes (chopped)

- 1 tablespoon tomato paste or tomato sauce

- 1 tablespoon ginger-garlic paste or 1/2 a teaspoon each of their powders

- 4-5 green chilies deseeded and slit into two ( optional )

- 2 potatoes (cut into quarters)

- 1 tablespoon curry powder

- 1 teaspoon paprika or chilly powder

- 1 teaspoon turmeric powder

- 1 tablespoon garam masala powder

- 2 bay leaves ( optional )

- 4-5 whole peppercorns

- 2-3 cloves

- 1 cinnamon stick , 1/4 teaspoon of its powder

- 3-4 green cardamoms ( optional)
- 2 tablespoons white vinegar


- 10-12 sprigs of coriander or parsley leaves or a pinch of dried herbs
- 3 tablespoons oil or ghee or butter
- 1 cup milk or reconstituted milk or coconut milk
- Salt to taste
- 1-2 cups warm water (as needed)

Method :

1. Marinate the mutton pieces with turmeric, paprika or chili powder, and salt. Let it rest for 1 hour.

2. Heat oil or butter or ghee in a large pan or pressure cooker. Add the bay leaves, if using , the peppercorns, cloves, cinnamon stick, and cardamoms if using . Sauté for a minute until the spices release their aroma.

3. Add the sliced onions and cilantro or parsley leaves or pinch of dried herbs Fry them until golden brown.

4. Add ginger-garlic paste: Stir in the ginger-garlic paste or their powders and fry for another 1 minute .

5. Add tomatoes and spices: Add the chopped tomatoes and cook until they soften. Then mix in curry powder , tomato paste or tomato sauce and garam masala. Cook for 2-3 minutes until the spices are well blended.

6. Add the marinated mutton pieces to the pan. Fry them on medium heat for 10 minutes, allowing the mutton to brown and absorb the spices.

7. Add the quartered potatoes and mix well. Add the vinegar .

8. Pour in enough water to cover the mutton and potatoes. If you're using a pressure cooker, cook for 15 minutes after the first

whistle . If using a regular pot, cover and simmer for 60 minutes until the mutton is tender, adding more water if necessary.

9. Once the mutton is cooked and tender, you can add milk or coconut milk for a richer flavor. Simmer for another 5 minutes to let the flavors blend.

10. Adjust seasoning and taste . Adjust the salt . Garnish with fresh cilantro leaves if needed ( optional )

Serve: This Railway Mutton Curry pairs well with steamed or cooked rice, flat breads , warm buns or heated crusty bread.

## 6 . COUNTRY CAPTAIN CHICKEN

Marinate : 30 minutes . Preparation and cooking time: 40 minutes

Ingredients:

- 1 kg chicken (cut into pieces)
- 2 onions (finely sliced)
- 2 tomatoes (chopped)
- 1 tablespoon ginger-garlic paste or 1/2 a teaspoon each of their powders
- 1 teaspoon turmeric powder
- 1 level tablespoon paprika or red chili powder
- 1 /2 level tablespoon curry powder powder
- 1 teaspoon garam masala
- 10-12 sprigs of cilantro or parsley leaves or a pinch of dried herbs

- 2-3 tablespoons oil , butter or ghee
- Few roasted nuts of your choice ( optional )
- 1/2 to 1 cup of yoghurt or a small cup of buttermilk or 1 cup milk

- Cilantro leaves (for garnish) or a pinch of dried herbs

- Salt and pepper (to taste)

- 1 tablespoon lemon juice ( optional )

Method :

1. In a bowl, mix the chicken pieces with turmeric, paprika or red chili powder, salt and pepper . Let it marinate for 30 minutes.

2. In a large pan, heat oil. Once hot, add the sliced onions. Fry the onions until golden brown.

3. Stir in the ginger-garlic paste or its powder and fry for about 2 minutes .

4.Add the chopped tomatoes and cook until they become soft and start to release oil.

5. Mix in the curry powder and garam masala. Cook for another minute. Add the lemon juice if using .

6.Add the marinated chicken to the pan. Fry on medium heat for 5-6 minutes, allowing the chicken to brown slightly.

7. Add a cup water to prevent sticking (if needed) and cover the pan. Let it simmer on low heat for 20-25 minutes, stirring occasionally, until the chicken is cooked through.

8.Once the chicken is cooked, adjust the seasoning, add the yoghurt or buttermilk or milk and garnish with fresh cilantro leaves and roasted nuts if using .

Serve: Country Captain Chicken is best enjoyed with a light salad or yoghurt , steamed rice, flatbread , bun toasted bread, or chapatis.


7.RAY FISH CURRY

Preparation and cooking time 45 minutes

Level : Medium hard

Ingredients:
- 500g ray fish (cleaned and cut into pieces)
- ½ teaspoon turmeric powder
- ½ teaspoons salt
- 1 tbsp lemon juice
- 2 tablespoons oil (coconut oil or vegetable oil)
- 1 onion, finely chopped
- 2 garlic cloves, minced or 1/2 teaspoon of its powder
- 1-inch piece of ginger, grated or 1/2 teaspoon of its powder
- 1 large tomato, chopped. Or 2 tablespoons of tomato sauce or its paste
- 1 teaspoon turmeric powder
- 1 teaspoon paprika or chili powder (adjust to taste)
- 1 teaspoon curry powder
- ½ teaspoon pepper powder
- 1 teaspoon mustard ( optional)
- 1 sprig cilantro or parsley leaves or a pinch of dried herbs
- 1 cup low fat milk or reconstituted milk or coconut milk
- 1 ½ cups warm water
- Salt to taste
- 2 tablespoons lemon juice or store bought tamarind paste ( dilute it in water )
- Fresh cilantro or parsley for garnish or a pinch of dried herbs .

Method :

1. Rub the ray fish with turmeric, salt, and lemon juice. Set aside to marinate for 30 minutes.

2. Heat oil in a pan for a few seconds.

3. Add the chopped onions and cook until golden brown.

4. Add the minced garlic, or its powder , grated ginger, or its powder . Sauté for 2 minutes.

5. Add the chopped tomatoes or the tomato paste or sauce and cook until they soften and blend into the mixture.

6. Add turmeric, chili or paprika powder, curry powder, and pepper powder. Stir and cook the spices for a few minutes.

7. Pour in the milk or coconut milk and water, stirring well to combine.

8. Bring the curry to a boil, then reduce the heat and let it simmer for 10 minutes.

9. Add the lemon juice or tamarind paste and salt. Stir well.

10. Gently place the marinated ray fish pieces into the simmering curry.

11. Cook for about 10 minutes, or until the fish is cooked through and tender. Avoid stirring too much to prevent the fish from breaking apart.

11.Once the fish is cooked, garnish with fresh cilantro or parsley , or a pinch of dried herbs.

This Anglo-Indian Ray Fish Curry, brings together mild spices and coconut-based flavors common in Anglo-Indian cuisine. Serve this with confidence with steamed rice or Hoppers ( app-am ) ( recipe in breakfast section ) , for a wholesome and flavorful meal.


## 8. SPICY OFFAL (Bovine Intestines) CURRY

Preparation and cooking time 1 hour

Level : Hard

Ingredients:

- 500 grams cow offal (intestines), cleaned and cut into pieces
- 2 large onions, finely chopped
- 2 tomatoes, chopped or 3 tablespoons of tomato paste or sauce
- 2 tablespoons ginger-garlic paste or 1/2 teaspoon each of their powders

- 1 teaspoon curry powder
- 5 peppercorns

- 4 cloves

- 1 piece cinnamon stick

- 1/2 teaspoon turmeric powder

- 1 teaspoon paprika or red chili powder

- 1/2 teaspoon garam masala

- 1/2 cup thick milk or reconstituted milk or yogurt for a richer curry

- 1/4 cup desiccated coconut, grated (optional)

- Fresh cilantro or parsley leaves or a two pinch of dried herbs for garnish

- Salt to taste

- Oil

Method:

1. Thoroughly clean the offal pieces. Boil them in water with a little salt for about 40 minutes until tender. Drain . Discard stock . Slice into small pieces when cool and set aside.

2. Heat oil in a large pan. Add chopped onions and cook until golden brown. Stir in ginger-garlic paste or their powders and cook until fragrant. Add the desiccated coconut and fry until brown but not burnt .

3. Add chopped tomatoes, or tomato paste or tomato sauce , Curry powder, turmeric powder, paprika or red chili powder, and salt. Cook until the tomatoes or sauce are soft and the oil starts to separate from the mixture.

4. Add the boiled , sliced offal pieces to the pan. Stir well to coat with the spices. Cook for 5 minutes, allowing the offal to absorb the flavors.

5. Add the milk or yogurt, mixing well. Add 1/2 cup of warm water to reach desired consistency. Simmer for 15 minutes on low heat until the curry thickens and the flavors combine

6. Stir in garam masala and rest it for an additional 5 minutes.

7. Garnish with fresh cilantro or parsley leaves or two pinch of dried herbs and serve hot with steamed or cooked rice , warmed rolls or flat bread like roti, plain naan or Pita bread .

This curry has rich, robust flavors and is a traditional dish enjoyed in Anglo-Indian cuisine , especially prepared for weddings , feasts and other celebrations .

## 9. CHICKEN LIVER CURRY

Preparation and cooking time 45 minutes

Level: Easy

Ingredients:

- 500 grams chicken liver, cleaned and trimmed
- 2 large onions, finely chopped
- 2 tomatoes, chopped or 2 tablespoons of tomato paste or sauce
- 2 tablespoons ginger-garlic paste or 1/2 teaspoon each of its powder
- 1 teaspoon pepper
- 1 teaspoon curry powder
- 1/2 teaspoon turmeric powder
- 1 teaspoon paprika or red chili powder
- 1/2 teaspoon garam masala

- 1/2 cup milk or reconstituted milk or coconut milk

- Fresh cilantro or parsley leaves or a pinch of dried herbs for garnish
- Salt to taste
- Oil for cooking

Method:

1. Clean the chicken liver thoroughly, removing any connective tissue or fat. Set aside.

2. Heat oil in a large pan over medium heat. Add the chopped onions and cook until golden brown.

3. Stir in ginger-garlic paste or their powders and cook about a minute until fragrant

4. Add chopped tomatoes, or tomato sauce , curry powder, turmeric powder, paprika or red chili powder, pepper and salt. Cook until the tomatoes are softened or sauce is cooked and the oil begins to separate from the mixture.

5. Add the chicken liver pieces to the pan. Stir well to coat with the spices Add a cup of water and cook on low heat for about 20 minutes until the liver is cooked through. Stir occasionally to ensure even cooking.

6. Stir in the milk or coconut milk, and cook for another 5 minutes. This will give the curry a creamy texture.

7. Sprinkle garam masala over the curry and cook for an additional 2 minutes to blend the flavors.

8. Garnish with fresh cilantro or parsley, or a pinch of dried herbs and serve hot with steamed or cooked rice, any flatbread like roti, or naan , or just simply with bun or lightly toasted bread or rolls .

This recipe offers a rich and flavorful curry that's typical of Anglo-Indian cuisine.


## 10. SHEEP / BEEF LIVER CURRY

Preparation and cooking time 45 minutes

Level : Medium hard

Ingredients:

- 500 grams beef or lamb liver, cleaned and cut into pieces

- 2 large onions, finely chopped

- 1 cooked potato cubed ( optional )

- 2 tomatoes, chopped or 2 tablespoons of tomato sauce

- 2 tablespoons ginger-garlic paste or 1/2 teaspoon each of their powders

- 1 teaspoon pepper

- 1 teaspoon curry powder

- 1/2 teaspoon turmeric powder

- 1/2 teaspoon garam masala

- 1 cup milk or reconstituted milk, or coconut milk

- Fresh cilantro or parsley leaves or a pinch of dried herbs for garnish

- Salt to taste

- Oil for cooking

Method:

1. Clean and cut the liver into pieces. Boil in water for about 10 minutes to make it tender. Drain and set aside. Reserve stock . Cook the potato , if using , and cube it

2. Heat oil in a large pan. Salute the aromatics . Add chopped onions and cook until golden brown. Stir in ginger-garlic paste or its powder and cook for a minute

3. Add chopped tomatoes, or tomato sauce , curry powder, turmeric powder, and salt. Cook until the tomatoes or sauce is soft and the oil begins to separate.

4.Add the boiled liver pieces to the pan. Add 2 tablespoons of the stock . Stir to coat with the spices , add the cooked potato if using , and cook for about 5 minutes.

5. Add the milk or coconut milk, Simmer on low heat for 20 minutes until the curry thickens and the flavors combine

6. Add garam masala and let it rest for another 5 minutes.

7. Garnish with fresh cilantro or parsley leaves or a pinch of dried herbs and serve hot with steamed or cooked rice , warm rolls , flatbread or sliced bread.

This recipe is a typical weekly staple of Anglo Indian diet , the robust flavor of this dish is typical of Anglo-Indian cuisine and is perfect for a hearty weekend meal.

## 11. SARDINE CURRY ( FUSION DISH )

Preparation and cooking time
Level : Somewhat hard
Ingredients:
- 500g Sardines
- 1onion or 5 shallots
- 2 small tomatoes or 2 tablespoons tomato paste or sauce

  - 1/2 teaspoon garlic powder
  - 1/2 teaspoon ginger powder (optional )
  - 1/2 teaspoon turmeric powder
  - 1 level teaspoon paprika or red chili powder

- 1/2 teaspoon pepper powder

  - Lemon juice ( 1/2 a lemon )
  - Milk or reconstituted milk or coconut milk,
  - Salt and pepper to taste
  - 1 tablespoon oil

Method:
1. Clean the sardines and set aside.
2. Heat oil in a pan and sauté finely chopped onions, ginger if using , until golden
3. Add chopped tomatoes or the sauce , garlic powder , turmeric, paprika or red chili powder, and pepper powder cooking until the tomatoes soften or the sauce cooks .

4. Add milk or coconut milk, and salt simmering to form a creamy curry base.

5. Add the sardines to the curry, cover, and cook on medium heat about 15 minutes until the fish is done, ensuring the curry is well-seasoned.

6. Serve hot with steamed or cooked rice or flat bread . This dish is a staple every month in Anglo Indian households and the type of fish used may vary according to seasons .


## 12. Vindaloo

Preparation and cooking time 1 hour

Level : Hard

Ingredients:

- 500g pork (or chicken or beef), sliced or cubed
- 2 large onions, finely sliced
- 2 tomatoes, chopped
- 6-8 garlic cloves, minced or 1/2 a teaspoon of its powder
- a piece of ginger, grated or 1/2 a teaspoon of its powder
- 1 tablespoon of paprika or red chill powder (add more for hotter spice),
- 2 tablespoon tomato paste or sauce
- 1/2 teaspoon level cinnamon powder

- 1 teaspoon black pepper powder
- 1 teaspoon mustard

- 2 tablespoon vinegar (white or malt)
- 1 teaspoon turmeric powder
- 1 teaspoon garam masala ( optional )
- 4-5 cloves or 1/4 teaspoon of its powder ( optional )
- 2 tablespoon oil

- Salt to taste
- 2 cups water

- Fresh cilantro , parsley chopped for garnish or a pinch of dried herbs

Method :

1.  In a non stick pan, add the oil and chopped onions , garlic and ginger and sauté 5 minutes on low heat until golden .

1.  Add the black pepper , chili or paprika powder , garam masala if using , turmeric , mustard , cinnamon and cloves or their powders , tomato paste or sauce , vinegar and sauté for a minute on low heat until fragrant . The oil should separate from the sauce

3. Add the meat cubes and brown them on all sides for about 5 minutes on medium heat

3. Pour in water, salt to taste, cover, and simmer for 30-40 minutes, on low heat stirring occasionally until the meat is tender and the sauce thickens. The meat should not burn . The sauce should be thick and not watery .

4. Add the chopped cilantro or parsley or the pinch of dried herbs and adjust seasoning.

4.Serve hot with roasted rice sautéed vegetables (optional ) steamed or cooked rice , flatbread or warm bread.

This authentic version offers a balanced heat level, with the option to adjust the chili powder to taste.


# 13 . CHICKPEA CURRY

Preparation and cooking time : Soak time overnight , cooking time 45 minutes
Level : Easy
Ingredients :

- 1 cup of chick peas soaked overnight in water . Or drain a can of chick peas .

- 1 cup milk or reconstituted milk or coconut milk

- 1 Tablespoon tomato paste or sauce or ketchup

- 1 chopped tomato ( optional )

- 2 cloves or 1/4 teaspoons of its powder

- 1 stick cinnamon or 1/2 teaspoon of its powder

- 1 teaspoon chopped garlic or 1/2 teaspoon of its powder

- 1 teaspoon garam masala or curry powder

- 1/2 teaspoon turmeric powder

- 2 tablespoons oil or butter

- 2 sprigs chopped cilantro or parsley or a pinch of dried herbs

- Salt and pepper to taste

**Method :**

1. Cook the chicken peas ( which was soaked overnight ) on medium heat 40 min or in a pressure cooker 25 min . Reserve 1 cup stock . If using from a can , drain off the water and set aside .

1. Sauté the onion in the oil . Sauté the cloves and cinnamon or its powder . Lower the heat and add garlic , turmeric , pepper , curry powder and the tomato paste or sauce . Sauté one minute . Add chopped tomato , if using .
2. Add the cup of milk and the chick peas with one cup of its cooked stock . If using from a can , add 1/2 cup of water more
3. Bring to a boil and simmer on low heat for 15 min with the herbs until the sauce is thick and syrupy . Adjust seasonings.
4. Serve with steamed or cooked rice , warm rolls or flatbread , with tomato salad or yoghurt ( optional )

CHAPTER SEVEN
SALADS

## 1.  POTATO AND EGG SALAD MILDLY SPICED

Preparation and cooking time 45 minutes
Level : Easy
Ingredients:
- 3 large potatoes, boiled and cubed
- 3 hard-boiled eggs, sliced
- 1 small onion, finely chopped
- 2 tablespoons mayonnaise
- 1 tablespoon plain yogurt or buttermilk ( optional )
- 1 teaspoon curry powder
- ½ teaspoon mustard
- 1 tablespoon lemon juice
- Fresh cilantro or parsley leaves, chopped or a pinch of dried herbs
- Salt and pepper to taste
Method:

1.  Boil the potatoes until cooked . When cool peel and cube them

1.  Boil the eggs 15 minutes until hard boiled . Dunk in ice cold water for ten minutes . Peel and slice them

3. In a large bowl, mix mayonnaise, yogurt, if using , curry powder, lemon juice, salt, and pepper.

4. Add the boiled potatoes, boiled sliced eggs, chopped onion, and the mustard . Mix gently.

5. Garnish with chopped cilantro or parsley leaves or a pinch of dried herbs and serve chilled.

Note : A teaspoon of grated Parmesan cheese may be added for a cheesy flavor ( optional) .


## 2. CHICKPEA AND TOMATO SALAD

Preparation and cooking time 25 min

Level : Easy

Ingredients:

- 1 can (400g) chickpeas, drained and rinsed with clean water

- 2 medium tomatoes, chopped

- 1 small cucumber, chopped

-1 tablespoon tomato sauce or ketchup

- one small onion chopped ( optional )

- 1 tablespoon chopped cilantro or mint or parsley mint leaves or a pinch of dried herbs

- ½ teaspoon black pepper powder

- 1 tablespoon lemon juice

- Salt to taste

Method:

1. In a bowl, combine chickpeas, chopped tomatoes, chopped onion and cucumber

2. Add pepper powder, tomato sauce , salt, and black pepper. Mix well.

3. Drizzle lemon juice over the salad and toss to coat.

4. Garnish with mint leaves. Serve chilled or at room temperature.

Note : A tablespoon of olive oil may be added ( optional )


## 3. PINEAPPLE AND CABBAGE SALAD

Preparation and cooking time 30 minutes

Level : Easy

Ingredients:

-1 cup pineapple, chopped fresh or drained from a can

You can substitute with 1 cup chopped apple or any other firm fruit

- 2 cups shredded cabbage ( steam shredded cabbage with a tablespoon of water for 1 min in a bowl in the microwave or 5 min in a steamer

- 1 small onion, thinly sliced

- 1 tablespoon raisins or sultanas ( optional )

- 1 tablespoon chopped roasted peanuts (optional)

- 1 teaspoon mustard

- 1 tablespoon olive oil or coconut oil

- 1 tablespoon apple cider vinegar or lemon juice

- Salt and pepper to taste

Method:

1. In a large bowl, combine pineapple, shredded cabbage, onion, and raisins if using

3. Add mustard , apple cider vinegar or lemon juice, salt, and pepper. Toss to mix.

4. Sprinkle chopped peanuts on top for extra crunch. Serve fresh.

Note : A tablespoon of mayonnaise may be added For extra flavor ( optional )

## 4. SIMPLE TOMATO AND ONION SALAD

Preparation and cooking time 15 minutes

Level : Easy

- 2 ripe tomatoes halved and sliced crosswise

- 1 onion sliced crosswise and the rings separated
- 1 tablespoon vinegar or lemon juice
- Salt and pepper to taste
- A sprig of cilantro or parsley or a pinch of dried herbs ( optional )

Method :

Combine all ingredients together . Keep for five minutes.

Serve with other main dishes either chilled or at room temperature. Should be used within the day .

## 5. BEETROOT , ONION POTATO SALAD

Preparation and cooking time 45 minutes

Level : Medium hard

Ingredients :

- 1 beetroot cooked and sliced ( or sliced beets from a can , drained )

- 1 potato boiled and sliced crosswise

- 1 small chopped onion

- 100g of cubed cottage cheese or feta , or any firm cheese that can be eaten uncooked

- 1 tablespoon lemon juice or vinegar

- 1 tablespoons olive oil or coconut oil ( optional )

- A tablespoon of mayonnaise

- A pinch of dried herbs ( optional )

- Salt and pepper to taste

Method :

- Boil the potato and slice it

- Boil the beet and slice it . Alternatively drain sliced beets from a can .

- Combine gently sliced beets , sliced potatoes , cubed cheese , chopped onion , lemon or vinegar , the olive oil, if using , the dried herbs , if using , salt and pepper to taste
.

- Add the mayonnaise

- Serve chilled or st room temperature with any type of lunch or dinner dish , or simply on its own . Should be eaten within the day .

## 6. THE GLORIOUS MASHED POTATO
Preparation and cooking time 45 min
Level : Easy
Ingredients :

- 2 large potatoes or three medium ones
- 1 tablespoon softened butter
- 2 tablespoon milk or reconstituted milk
- Salt and pepper to taste

Method :

1.  Boil the potatoes . Remove skins .Cool and mash them
    with the softened butter salt and pepper to taste and the
    milk .

1.  Form into a rectangle or circular shape and chill
2.  Serve on its own or with extra melted butter or grated
    Parmesan cheese ( optional ) , with a dollop of mayonnaise
    ( optional ) or with main lunch dishes . These salads offer
    Anglo-Indian twist, blending traditional flavors like
    mustard , lemon juice , pepper , with other familiar
    ingredients.

# CHAPTER EIGHT
# TEA TIME SNACKS
# 1. MINCED BEEF SAMOSAS , FUSION SNACK

Preparation and cooking time 1 hour

Level : Somewhat hard

- Ingredients:

- 500g Minced beef,

- 1 onion

- 2 green chilies deseeded ( optional)

- ginger-garlic paste or half a teaspoon each of ginger garlic paste

- 1/2 a teaspoon of turmeric,

- 1/2 a teaspoon of garam masala,

- A few sprigs of cilantro or parsley or a pinch of dried herbs

- 2 cups of all purpose flour,

- Warm water as needed

- Salt and pepper to taste

- Oil for frying and sauté

Method:

1. Heat oil in a pan and sauté chopped onions, green chilies if using , and ginger-garlic paste or powders , cooking until golden.

2. Add the minced beef, turmeric, garam masala, and salt, and half a cup of water , cooking until the beef is browned and cooked through. Around ten minutes. Stir in chopped cilantro leaves / parsley or the herbs

3. Prepare dough by mixing flour, salt, and water, rolling it out into thin circles. The diameter should be half of a large tortilla .

4. Place a spoonful of the beef mixture in the center of each circle, fold into a triangle, and seal the edges by pressing them with fingers dipped in water

5. Heat a wok or pan with 2cm of oil and Deep fry the samosas in medium heat until golden brown. Drain on paper towels or metal strainer .

6. Serve hot with chutney or ketchup. This is a perfect tea time snack .

This snack can be filled with just cottage cheese or any crumbly cheese instead of minced beef , for a different variety . In that case no spices no sautéing either . The rest of the steps will be same .


## 2. CRAB CAKES

Preparation and cooking time 45 minutes

Level : Medium hard

Ingredients:

- 500 grams crab meat either cooked and picked without shell bits or alternatively crab meat from 2 small cans which should be steamed for ten minutes or cooked

- 1/2 cup breadcrumbs

- 1/4 cup finely chopped onions

- 1/4 cup finely chopped green bell pepper

- 2 green chilies, deseeded finely chopped (optional)

- 1 tablespoon ginger-garlic paste or half a teaspoon each of their powder

- 1 teaspoon paprika

- 1/2 teaspoon turmeric powder

- 1/2 teaspoon garam masala

- 1 egg (beaten)
- 1 large potato cooked and mashed with a spoon

- 2 tablespoons chopped cilantro or parsley or a pinch of dried herbs
- Salt to taste
- Oil for frying
Method:

1.  Boil the potato and mash it .

1.  In a bowl, combine cooked crab meat, mashed potato , breadcrumbs, chopped onions, bell pepper, green chilies, ginger-garlic paste, or powder , paprika turmeric powder, garam masala, beaten egg, and salt. Mix well to form a uniform mixture, that can be shaped
2.  Form the mixture into 1/2 inch thick patties or cakes, the size of a round biscuit
3.  Heat oil in a non stick pan over medium heat. Fry the crab cakes until golden brown and crispy on both sides, about 3-4 only minutes per side.

5. Remove from the pan and drain on paper towels.
Serve the crab cakes hot with a side of ketchup or tartar sauce or chutney.


## 3. EGG PUFFS

Preparation and cooking 45 minutes
Level : Medium hard
Ingredients:
- 4 hard-boiled eggs, halved
- 1 onion, finely sliced

- 1 teaspoon ginger-garlic paste or 1/2 teaspoon each of their powder
- 1/2 teaspoon turmeric powder
- 1/2 teaspoon garam masala powder
- 1 tablespoon tomato paste or sauce
- Salt, to taste
- 1 sheet puff pastry, thawed
- 1 egg, beaten (for egg wash)
- 2 tablespoons oil
- Fresh cilantro or parsley leaves, chopped or a pinch of dried herbs

Method :

1. Heat oil in a pan and sauté the onions, and ginger-garlic paste or their powders until golden.

2. Add the turmeric, tomato sauce or paste and garam masala powders. Mix well and cook until fragrant . Turn off the heat . Add salt and cilantro or parsley leaves, or the dried herbs and let the mixture cool.

3. Roll out the puff pastry sheet and cut it into squares. Place a spoonful of the onion mixture in the center of each square.

4. Place half a boiled egg on top of the onion mixture, and fold the pastry over to seal.

5. Brush the tops with beaten egg, and bake in a preheated oven at 375°F (190°C) or in an air fryer lined with heat proof liner at 180°C for about 20 minutes or until golden brown.

6. Serve hot with ketchup or tomato sauce or a yoghurt dip


## 4. SPICED POTATO BALLS

Preparation and cooking time 45 minutes
Level : Medium hard
Ingredients:

- 2 large potatoes, boiled and mashed
- 1 onion, finely chopped
- 1 tablespoon tomato sauce or paste
- 1 teaspoon ginger-garlic paste or 1/2 teaspoon each of their powders
- 1/2 teaspoon turmeric powder
- 1/2 teaspoon mustard ( optional)
- A sprig of cilantro or parsley leaves or a pinch of dried herbs
- Salt, to taste
- Oil for frying
- For the batter:
- 1 cup chickpea flour ( gram flour )
- 1/2 teaspoon turmeric powder
- 1/2 teaspoon paprika or red chili powder
- 1/2 teaspoon of black pepper
- Salt, to taste
- Water, as needed

Method :

1. In a pan, heat some oil and add onions, and cilantro or parsley or herbs .Sauté until golden.

2. Add ginger-garlic paste or their powder , mustard and turmeric powder, and tomato paste and cook until fragrant

3. Add the mashed potatoes, salt Mix well and allow to cool. Shape the mixture into small balls.

4.Make a very thick syrupy batter with the chickpea flour and batter ingredients.

5. Heat 1 inch depth of oil in a pan . Coat the potato balls in the batter and fry them in medium heat until golden . Drain on paper towels and serve with tomato sauce , or a yoghurt dip .


## 5 .APPLE SAUCE TART TOPPED WITH JAM

Preparation and cooking time 1 hour

Level : Hard

Ingredients:

For the Tart Base:

- 1 ½ cups all-purpose flour

- ½ cup cold butter, diced

- 2 tablespoon powdered sugar

- 1 egg yolk


  - 1-2 tablespoons cold water

  - For the Apple Sauce:


- 4 large apples (peeled, cored, and chopped)

- ¼ cup sugar (adjust this to taste)

- ½ teaspoon cinnamon powder

- ½ cup water

For the Jam Topping:

- 3-4 tablespoons mixed fruit jam or any jam of choice

Method :

For the Tart Base:

1. Preheat the oven to 180°C (350°F).

2. In a bowl, mix the flour and powdered sugar.

3. Rub the cold butter into the flour until it forms a breadcrumb-like texture.

4. Add the egg yolk and a tablespoon of cold water. Mix gently until it forms a dough. Add more water if needed.

5. Roll the dough into a ball, wrap it in plastic, and chill for 20 minutes.

6. Roll out the dough and press it into a tart tin. Trim the edges to fit

7. Prick the base with a fork and bake in the preheated oven for 20 minutes or until golden brown. Let it cool.

For the Apple Sauce:

1. In a saucepan, add the chopped apples, sugar, cinnamon powder, and water.

2. Cook over medium heat, stirring occasionally, until the apples soften (about 15 minutes).

3. Once soft, mash or cook and blend the apples to create a smooth sauce. Let it cool.

4. Once the tart base has cooled, spread the apple sauce evenly over it.

5. Gently spoon the jam on top of the apple sauce.

6. Serve chilled or at room temperature.

This tart combines the sweet and tangy flavors of apple sauce with the richness of jam, perfect for an Anglo-Indian afternoon tea and is regularly prepared on a weekly basis in Anglo Indian households.


## 6. STANDARD BAKED APPLE PIE

Preparation and cooking time 2 hours

Level : Hard

Ingredients:

For the Pie Crust:

- 2 ½ cups all-purpose flour

- 1 cup cold butter, diced

- 1 tablespoon sugar

- 1 teaspoon salt

- 6-8 tablespoon ice-cold water

- 1 egg (for egg wash)

For the Apple Filling:

- 6 medium-sized apples (peeled, cored, and thinly sliced)

- ½ cup sugar (adjust this to taste)

- 2 tablespoon brown sugar

- 1 teaspoon cinnamon powder

- 1 tablespoon lemon juice
- 2 tablespoon flour (to thicken the filling)
- 1 tablespoon butter (cut into small pieces)

Method :

For the Pie Crust:

1. In a large bowl, mix the flour, sugar, and salt.

2. Cut in the cold butter using a pastry cutter or your fingers until the mixture resembles coarse bread crumbs.

3. Gradually add the ice-cold water, 1 tablespoon at a time, and mix until the dough just comes together. Do not overwork the dough.

4. Divide the dough into two equal parts, form into discs, wrap in plastic wrap, and refrigerate for at least 30 minutes.

For the Apple Filling:

1. In a large bowl, toss the apple slices with sugar, brown sugar, cinnamon, lemon juice, and flour until well coated.

2. Let the mixture sit for 10 minutes to allow the apples to release some juice.

Assemble and bake the Pie

1. Preheat the oven to 190°C (375°F).

2. On a floured surface, roll out one disc of the chilled dough to fit a 9-inch pie pan, leaving an overhang at the edges.

3. Press the dough into the pie pan and trim the edges, leaving about ½ inch overhang. Scallop the edges using your fingers or a fork

4. Fill the pie crust with the prepared apple filling, dot the top with small pieces of cold butter.

5. Roll out the second disc of dough to cover the top. Place it over the apples and seal the edges by crimping them with a fork or spoon .

6. Cut a few small slits in the top crust to allow steam to escape during baking.

7. Brush the top with an egg wash (1 egg with 1 tbsp water) for a golden finish.

8. Bake in the preheated oven for 45-55 minutes, or until the crust is golden brown and the apples are tender. Check in between as this timing depends on your oven .

9. Let the pie cool for at least 1 hour before slicing.

This Sweet Baked Apple Pie has buttery, flaky crust and aromatic apple filling . It's usually prepared during weekends and family gatherings .

7. Butter Biscuits

Preparation and cooking time 40 minutes

Level : Medium hard

Ingredients:

- 1 cup all-purpose flour

- 1/2 cup unsalted butter, softened

- 1/4 cup sugar

- 1/4 teaspoon baking powder

- 1/4 teaspoon salt

- 1/2 teaspoon vanilla extract (optional)

- 1-2 tablespoons milk (as needed)

Method:

1. In a bowl, cream together the butter and sugar until light and fluffy. Mix in the vanilla extract if using.

2. In a separate bowl, whisk together flour, baking powder, and salt.

3. Gradually add the dry ingredients to the butter mixture, mixing until a soft dough forms. If the dough is too dry, add milk a tablespoon at a time until it comes together.

4. Roll out the dough on a lightly floured surface to about 1/4 inch thickness. Cut into desired shapes using cookie cutters.

5. Place the biscuits on a baking sheet lined with parchment paper. Bake in a preheated oven at 180°C (350°F) for 10-12 minutes or until the edges are golden brown.

6. Allow to cool on a wire rack before serving.


8. Spiced Biscuits ( Fusion recipe )

Preparation and cooking time 40 minutes

Level: Medium hard

Ingredients:

- 1 cup all-purpose flour
- 1/2 cup unsalted butter, softened
- 1/4 cup sugar
- 1/2 tablespoon caraway seeds or its powder
- 1/4 teaspoon baking powder
- 1/4 teaspoon salt
- 1 egg (optional, for egg wash)

Method:

1. In a bowl, cream the butter and sugar until light and fluffy. Add the caraway seeds and mix well.

2. In another bowl, mix flour, baking powder, and salt.

3. Gradually add the dry ingredients to the butter mixture, mixing until a soft dough forms. If needed, use a little milk to bring the dough together.

4. Roll out the dough on a floured surface to about 1/4 inch thickness. Cut into rounds or desired shapes. If desired, brush the tops with a beaten egg for a glossy finish.

5. Place on a baking sheet lined with parchment paper. Bake in a preheated oven at 180°C (350°F) for 12-15 minutes or until golden brown.

6. Cool and Serve: Cool on a wire rack before serving.

## 9. Coconut Cookies ( Fusion Recipe )

Preparation and cooking time 40 minutes

Level : Medium hard

Ingredients:

- 1 cup all-purpose flour
- 1 cup desiccated coconut
- 1/2 cup unsalted butter, softened
- 1/2 cup sugar
- 1/4 teaspoon baking powder
- 1/4 teaspoon baking soda
- 1/4 teaspoon salt
- 1/2 teaspoon vanilla extract (optional)
- 1 egg

Method:

1. Preheat your oven to 180°C (350°F) and line a baking sheet with parchment paper.

2. In a bowl, cream together the butter and sugar until light and fluffy. Mix in the egg and vanilla extract if using.

3. In a separate bowl, sift together the flour, baking powder, baking soda, and salt. Stir in the desiccated coconut.

4. Gradually add the dry ingredients to the butter mixture, mixing until just combined. The dough will be thick. Roll the dough into small balls and place them on the prepared baking sheet, flattening them slightly with your fingers.

5. Bake for 10-12 minutes, or until the edges are golden brown.

6. Allow the cookies to cool on the baking sheet for a few minutes before transferring them to a wire rack to cool completely.


## 10. CHEWY CHOCOLATE COOKIE

Preparation and cooking time 45 min

Level : Medium hard

Ingredients :

- 1.5 cups of all purpose flour
- 1 cup of sugar
- 4 teaspoons of dark chocolate powder
- 1/2 cup of softened butter
- 1 egg beaten
- A pinch of baking powder
- 2 or 3 tablespoons of water or milk
- 1/2 a teaspoon of vanilla extract

Method :

1. Preheat the air fryer or oven to 175°C

1. Combine the sugar and the butter with a small whisk until creamy .
2. Add the beaten egg , vanilla extract and the pinch of baking powder
3. Combine flour with the chocolate powder in a bowl
4. Add the flour little at a time with a few tablespoons of water until a thick consistency is reached . It should fall like a moist lump from the whisk . It should not be fluid fluid . It should not be flowing . Adjust the spoons of water as required
5. Grease two squares or circles of parchment or baking paper with a little butter and divide this batter into both . Form with a spoon into one circle or rectangle . Do not cut .
6. Bake the first one in a air fryer or oven for 12 minutes until cooked and a tooth pick comes out clean from the middle . The inside and the top will move slightly like a chewy cookie . Cool on a rack for 15 minutes .

1. Bake the second portion the same way . Cool on rack 15 minutes . Store in a wide cookie tin or container , and slice only when required and use within a week . Adjust timings according to the type of oven used .

Note : For those who desire , roasted nuts may be added to the batter while mixing

Enjoy these cookies at tea or leisure times.

## 11. SIMPLE SWEET RICE PORRIDGE

Preparation and cooking time 45 minutes
Level : Medium hard
Ingredients :

- 1 cup cooked or steamed rice ( mashed )
- 3 tablespoons sugar
- One pinch of cinnamon
- 2 cups of milk or reconstituted milk or coconut milk
- 1 tablespoon butter or ghee

Method :

1. Cook or steam the rice until soft . Any soft rice like basmati rice . Mash it well .

1. Heat a small casserole . Add the butter or ghee on low heat
2. Add the sugar and the milk . Heat on low fire until sugar is melted
3. Add the pinch of cinnamon and the cooked mashed rice .
4. Stir without lumps , until the porridge is heated through .
5. Turn off the heat and serve as a sweet dessert .

Note : Chopped nuts or raisins may be added for extra flavor ( optional )

## 12. SWEET VERMICELLI SOUP

Preparation and cooking time 45 minutes

Level : Medium hard

Ingredients :

- 1 cup vermicelli broken
- 3-4 table spoons sugar
- 2 cups of milk
- 1 tablespoon butter or ghee
- One pinch of cinnamon
- 1 cup water or as needed

Method :

1. Heat a medium casserole on low heat . Add the butter or ghee and the broken vermicelli . Sauté until the vermicelli starts to turn light brown .

1. Add 1 cup of water and cook the vermicelli on low heat until cooked . Check frequently and add water by spoonfuls as required , until all the water is absorbed and the vermicelli is cooked

2. Add the sugar and once it melts add the milk and pinch of cinnamon .

3. Stir slowly on low heat until it comes to a simmer and becomes a liquid cream consistency , but not so thick .

4. Turn off the heat , let it rest 5 minutes and serve warm or hot as a dessert .

Note : Toasted chopped nuts or raisins may be added for those who prefer it ( optional )

# CHAPTER nine
# FRITTERS

## 1. SMALL DOUGH FRITTERS

Preparation and cooking time 45 min

Ingredients:

- 2 cups all-purpose flour
- 1/4 cup sugar
- 1/4 teaspoon salt
- 2 teaspoons baking powder
- 2 large eggs
- 3/4 cup milk or reconstituted milk
- 1 teaspoon vanilla extract
- Vegetable oil for frying
- Sugar for dusting

Method :

1. In a bowl, mix the flour, sugar, salt, and baking powder.

2. In a separate bowl, whisk together the eggs, milk, and vanilla extract.

3. Gradually add the wet ingredients to the dry ingredients, stirring until smooth. The batter should be thick and fall slowly from a spoon . Adjust the milk accordingly .

4. Heat oil 1.5 centimeter deep in a frying pan over medium heat.

5. Drop tablespoonfuls of batter gently into the hot oil in twos or threes and fry until golden brown, turning as needed.

6. Remove from the oil, drain on paper towels, and dust with powdered sugar before serving.

# 2. Kal-Kals (Sweet Fried Fritters )

Preparation and Cooking time One hour or more

Level : Fairly hard

Ingredients:

- 2 cups all-purpose flour

- 1/4 cup sugar

- 1/4 teaspoon salt

- 1 teaspoon baking powder

- 2 tablespoons ghee (clarified butter) or butter

- 1/2 cup milk or reconstituted milk or coconut milk

- 1/4 teaspoon cardamom powder ( optional )

- Oil for frying

- Powdered sugar for dusting

Method :

1. In a large bowl, sift together the flour, sugar, salt, baking powder, and cardamom powder ( if using )

2. Add the ghee or softened butter to the dry ingredients and mix until the mixture resembles breadcrumbs.

3. Gradually add milk or coconut milk to form a soft, pliable dough. Knead the dough lightly.

4. Divide the dough into small balls, each about the size of a large marble

5. Roll each ball into a smooth bun and press it onto the back of a fork to create a ridged pattern.

6. Heat oil 1 inch deep in a deep frying pan over medium heat.

7. Fry the fritters in batches until they are golden brown and crispy on the outside.

8. Drain on paper towels and dust with powdered sugar while still warm.

9. Serve as a sweet treat or as a festive snack at Christmas season

.

## 3. MYSORE BUNS

Preparation and fermenting time 4-5 hours and cooking time 30 minutes

Level : Hard

Ingredients:

- 2 ripe bananas, mashed
- 2 cups all-purpose flour
- 1/4 cup sugar
- 1/4 teaspoon salt
- 1/2 teaspoon baking soda
- 2 tablespoons yogurt
- Oil for frying

Method :

1. In a large bowl, mix the mashed bananas, sugar, salt, and yogurt .

2. Add the baking soda and gradually mix in the flour to the banana mixture to form a soft dough. If the dough is too sticky, add a little more flour.

3. Cover the dough with a damp cloth and let it rest for at least 4-5 hours, for best results.

4. After resting, knead the dough lightly and divide it into small balls.

5. Roll each ball into a thick, round bun (about 1/4 inch thick). Puncture the middle slightly with the handle of a spoon

6. Heat oil in a deep frying pan over low heat.

7. Fry the buns one by one until they puff up and turn golden brown and cooked on both sides.

8. Lift up with slotted spoon . Drain on paper towels and serve hot with jam or as a snack on its own .

## 4. SAVILINGE (BANANA FLAVOR ) FRITTERS

Preparation and fermentation time 2 hours and cooking time 30 minutes

Level : Medium hard

Ingredients:

- 2 large ripe Robusta or any type of firm (not soft ) ripe bananas, mashed

- 1/4 cup liquid molasses or grated jaggery or dark sugar

- 1/4 cup sugar

- 1 teaspoon active dry yeast

- 1/4 cup warm water (to activate the yeast)

- 1 1/2 to 2 cups all-purpose flour (adjust to achieve the right consistency)

- A pinch of salt

- Oil for deep frying

Method :

1.  Dissolve the yeast in warm water with a teaspoon of sugar. Let it sit for about 5-10 minutes until it becomes frothy.

2.  In a large mixing bowl, combine the mashed bananas, molasses or jaggery, and sugar. Mix until the jaggery is well incorporated.

3.  Add the activated yeast to the banana mixture and mix well.

4.  Gradually add the flour and a pinch of salt, mixing until you get a thick but pourable batter. The batter should be thick enough to hold its shape when dropped from a spoon but should still fall easily but not fluid

5.  Cover the bowl with a damp cloth and let the batter rest in a warm place for 2 hours, or until it has risen and is slightly bubbly.

6. Heat oil 1 inch deep in a deep frying pan , over medium heat. Once the oil is hot, lower the heat and drop tablespoonfuls of the thick batter gently into the oil, being careful not to overcrowd the pan.

7. Fry the fritters until they are golden brown and crispy on all sides, turning them occasionally to ensure even cooking.

8. Remove the fritters with a slotted spoon and drain on paper towels.

9. Serve the Savilinge warm, as a comfort food , a dessert or as a fried snack . They can be enjoyed plain or with a sprinkle of powdered sugar or spread with fruit jam.

These fritters are sweet, soft, and full of banana flavor, making them a perfect treat for any time of day for banana lovers .


## 5. WHOLE SLICED BANANA FRITTERS

Preparation and cooking time 30 min

Level : Easy

Ingredients

- 4 Ripe and firm Robusta or any firm ripe bananas

- 2 tablespoons sugar

- A small pinch of cinnamon powder ( optional)

- A small pinch of salt

- 1 cup of flour

- 1/2 teaspoon of baking powder

- 1/2 cup Warm water

- Oil for frying

Method :

1, Peel and slice the bananas lengthwise.

2. Mix the flour with the pinch of salt , the sugar and the baking powder . Add warm water gradually and form into a thick syrupy batter with a whisk . Adjust water accordingly.

3. Heat 1 inch of oil in a frying pan in medium heat .

4. Dip each slit banana into the batter and fry two or three at a time , turning once until lightly golden. Lift with metal tongs into kitchen paper .

5. Serve on its own as a fritter for casual eating .

These Anglo-Indian fritters are perfect for festive times , offering a delightful combination of flavors and textures.

# CHAPTER TEN
# SANDWICHES
# 1. CHICKEN SANDWICH

Preparation and cooking time 20 minutes

Level : Easy

Ingredients:

- 2 slices of sliced bread (white or whole wheat)

- ½ cup cooked chicken, shredded or chopped

- 2 tablespoon mayonnaise

- 1 teaspoon mustard (optional)

- 1 teaspoon ketchup or tomato sauce

- Salt and pepper to taste

- 1-2 leaves of lettuce

- 1-2 slices of tomato

- 1 tablespoon butter (optional, for toasting)

Method :

1. In a bowl, mix the shredded cooked chicken with mayonnaise and mustard. Season with salt and pepper.

2. Spread the chicken mixture evenly over one slice of bread.

3. Add a lettuce leaf and tomato slices on top.

4. Spread ketchup thinly on the second slice . Cover with the second slice of bread.

5. Butter the outsides of both bread slices lightly. Heat a pan and toast the sandwich on both sides until golden brown, about 2-3 minutes per side. Toast the sandwich. ( optional )

6. Cut the sandwich diagonally and enjoy hot .

For a twist, you can add grated Parmesan , or cottage cheese ,or cream cheese on other half of the bread instead of ketchup . Use within the hour .


## 2 . PATE SANDWICH

Preparation and cooking time 20 minutes

Level : Easy

Ingredients:

- 2 slices of sliced bread (white or brown)
- 100g chicken liver pâté (or you can substitute with meat pâté)
- 1 tablespoon butter (softened)
- 1 teaspoon English mustard (optional)

- 2-3 slices of cucumber
- 1-2 slices of tomato
- 1 teaspoon of ketchup or tomato sauce
- Salt and pepper to taste

Method :

1. Lightly butter both slices of bread. For extra flavor, mix a little mustard into the butter.

2. Spread the pâté generously over one of the buttered slices. The other side spread thinly with ketchup or tomato sauce .

3. Place the cucumber and tomato slices with a little salt and pepper over the pâté.

4 . Place the other slice of bread on top to form the sandwich.

5 . Cut the sandwich diagonally and serve.

This recipe is perfect for tea time or as a light lunch. The richness of the pâté pairs well with the freshness of the vegetables, giving it that Anglo-Indian flair. Use within the hour .

Note : Instead of ketchup you can substitute with thinly spread cream cheese .


## 3 . CLASSIC CILANTRO CHUTNEY BUTTER SANDWICH

Preparation and cooking time 30 minutes

Level : Easy

Ingredients:

- 4 slices of white bread (or your preferred bread)

- 2 tablespoons butter (softened)

- 2-3 tablespoons green chutney (see recipe below)

For the Green Chutney:

- 1 cup fresh cilantro leaves

- ½ cup fresh mint or parsley leaves

- 1 tablespoon lemon juice

- 1 garlic clove or 1/4 teaspoon of its powder

- ½ inch ginger or 1/4 teaspoon of its powder

- ½ teaspoon sugar

- Salt to taste

Method:

1. In a blender , blend all the chutney ingredients together with a little water until smooth. It should not be watery . Set aside.

2. Spread butter on one side of each slice of bread.

- On the other side, spread a generous layer of green chutney.

- Place two slices together, with the chutney sides facing inward, and press lightly.

3. Cut the sandwich into triangles or squares and serve fresh. Use within the hour .

Note : Instead if the butter , it may be substituted with cream cheese .

4 .TOMATO , BUTTER AND GREEN CHUTNEY SANDWICH

Preparation and cooking time 30 minutes

Level : Easy

Ingredients:

- 4 slices of soft white or whole wheat bread

- 2 tablespoons butter (softened)

- 2-3 tablespoons cilantro chutney (see recipe below )

- 1 ripe tomato, thinly sliced

- Salt and pepper to taste

For the Cilantro Chutney:

- 1 cup cilantro leaves

- 1 garlic clove or 1/4 teaspoon of its powder

- 1 tablespoon lemon juice

- 1 teaspoon sugar

- Salt to taste

Method:

1. In a blender , Blend all the chutney ingredients with a little water to make a smooth paste. It should not be watery

2. Spread butter on one side of each slice of bread.

- On the other side, spread the cilantro chutney.

- Add thin tomato slices on top of the chutney.

- Sprinkle salt and pepper over the tomatoes.

- Close the sandwich, with the chutney sides facing inward.

3. Slice and serve fresh, optionally with tea or coffee. Use within the hour

Note : Cream cheese may be substituted for the butter

## 5. COTTAGE CHEESE SANDWICH

Preparation time 20 minutes

Level: Easy

Ingredients:
- 200g cottage cheese crumbled or grated
- 4 slices of bread (whole wheat or white)
- 1 tablespoon butter (softened)
- 1 small onion, finely chopped

- 1 small tomato, finely chopped
- 2 tablespoons fresh cilantro leaves, chopped

- Salt and pepper to taste
- Lemon juice, to taste

Method:

1. In a bowl, mix the crumbled or grated cottage cheese, chopped onion, tomato, and chopped cilantro leaves.

2. Season with salt, pepper Add a squeeze of lemon juice for a fresh, tangy flavor. Mix everything well to combine.

3. Spread butter on one side of each bread slice. On the other side, spread the cottage cheese mixture evenly.

4. Place the bread slices together with the cottage cheese mixture facing inward. Lightly press the sandwich together. Cut diagonally or into halves .You can serve it as it is , or better still , grill it before slicing , for a crispy version.

5. If you prefer a grilled sandwich, grill on a hot pan or sandwich maker until golden brown. ( Optional ). Use within the hour .

Enjoy this fresh, protein-packed sandwich as a quick breakfast or snack .


## 6. EGG AND CUCUMBER BUTTEREDSANDWICH

Preparation and cooking time 25 minutes

Level : Easy

Ingredients:
- 2 hard-boiled eggs, peeled and sliced
- 4 slices of bread (white, whole wheat, or multi-grain)
- 2 tablespoons butter (softened)
- ½ a cucumber, thinly sliced
- Salt and pepper to taste
- A pinch of mustard powder or ½ teaspoon mustard sauce (optional)

Method:

1. Hard-boil the eggs and let them cool before peeling. Slice them into rounds.

2. Thinly slice the cucumber.

3. Spread butter on one side of each bread slice.

4. On other slice, layer the sliced eggs. Sprinkle salt, pepper, and a pinch of mustard powder or spread mustard sauce for added flavor.

5. Layer the cucumber slices on top of the eggs.

6. Place the other buttered slices of bread on top, with the buttered sides facing inward. Lightly press the sandwich together.

7. Slice the sandwich diagonally or into halves . Use within the hour .

These sandwiches are a staple in many Anglo-Indian homes, quick to make, and perfect for a light snack.

# CHAPTER ELEVEN

( STEEPED ) TEAS

These are recipes for Anglo-Indian steeped clear beverages, which are refreshing and sometimes infused with a blend of spices like clove and cinnamon and herbs like mint , providing an aromatic start to the day or a calming effect later in the day .


## 1. GINGER AND LEMON TEA

Preparation and cooking time 20 minutes

Level : Easy

A soothing and refreshing drink, ginger and lime tea is perfect for any time of day.

Ingredients:

- 1-inch piece of fresh ginger, sliced

- 1 lime, sliced

- 4 cups water

- 1 tablespoon honey or sugar (optional) only for those who need

- Fresh mint leaves for garnish ( optional )

Method :

1. Boil the water in a pot.

2. Add the sliced ginger and simmer for 10 minutes.

3. Remove from heat and add the lime slices. Let it steep for 5 minutes.

4. Strain the tea into cups, sweeten with honey or sugar if desired, and garnish with fresh mint leaves. Serve hot or cold. This tea should be used within the day .

## 2 . MINT AND LEMONGRASS INFUSED TEA

This fragrant and refreshing drink is perfect for cooling down on a hot day.

Method :

- 2 stalks of fresh lemongrass, chopped

- A handful of fresh mint leaves

- 4 cups water

- 1 tablespoon honey or sugar (optional) only for those who need to sweeten

- Lime slices for garnish

Method :

1. Boil the water in a pot.

2. Add the chopped lemongrass and mint leaves, and let it simmer for 5 minutes.

3. Remove from heat and let it steep for an additional 10 minutes covered .

4. Strain the infusion into cups, sweeten with honey or sugar if desired, and garnish with lime slices. Serve hot or cold. This tea should be used within the day .


## 3. CINNAMON AND CARDAMOM TEA

A lightly spiced tea that combines the warmth of cardamom and cinnamon for a comforting beverage.

Ingredients:

- 4 green cardamom pods, crushed

- 1 cinnamon stick

- 4 cups water

- 1 tablespoon honey or sugar (optional)

- Lemon slices for garnish

Method :

1. Boil the water in a pot.

2. Add the crushed cardamom pods and cinnamon stick, and let it simmer for 10 minutes.

3. Remove from heat and let it steep for an additional 5 minutes.

4. Strain the tea into cups, sweeten with honey or sugar if desired, and garnish with lemon slices. Serve hot. This tea should be used within the day .

## 4. CLOVE AND CINNAMON SPICED TEA

Preparation and cooking time 20 minutes

Level : Easy

A robust and aromatic tea with the combined warmth of cinnamon and cloves, perfect for a chilly or rainy day.

Ingredients:

- 2 cinnamon sticks

- 4 cloves

- 4 cups water

- 2 tea bags or 2 tsp loose black tea

- 1 tablespoon honey or sugar (optional)

- Milk (optional)

Method :

1. Boil the water in a pot.

2. Add the cinnamon sticks and cloves, and simmer for 10 minutes to release the flavors.

3. Add the loose tea or tea bags and let it steep for 3-5 minutes.

4. Strain the tea into cups, sweeten with honey or sugar if desired, and add milk if preferred. Serve hot. This tea should be used within the day .

## 5. CINNAMON TEA

Preparation and cooking time 20 minutes

Level : Easy

A soothing tea that blends the spiciness of cinnamon with the aromatic notes of black tea

Ingredients:

- 1 cinnamon stick
- 4 cups water
- 2 tea bags or 2 tsp loose black tea

- 1 tablespoon honey or sugar (optional)

Method :

1. Bring the water to a boil in a pot.

2. Add the cinnamon stick . Simmer for 10 minutes.

3. Add the loose tea or tea bags and let it steep for 3-5 minutes.

4. Strain the tea into cups and sweeten with honey or sugar if desired. Serve hot with lemon wedges if desired .

## 6. CLOVE AND GINGER TEA

Preparation and cooking time 20 minutes

Level : Easy

This tea combines the spiciness of cloves and ginger, offering a warming and invigorating drink.

Ingredients:

- 4 cloves
- 1-inch piece of fresh ginger, sliced
- 4 cups water
- 2 teaspoon loose black tea or 2 tea bags
- 1 tablespoon honey or sugar (optional)
- Lemon slices for garnish

Method :

1. Boil the water in a pot.

2. Add the cloves and sliced ginger, and simmer for 10 minutes.

3. Add the loose tea or tea bags and let it steep for 3-5 minutes.

4. Strain the tea into cups, sweeten with honey or sugar if desired, and garnish with lemon slices. Serve hot.

## 7. CLOVE AND CINNAMON MASALA CHAI

Preparation and cooking time 20 min

Level : Easy

A traditional masala chai infused with cloves and cinnamon, offering a spicy and fragrant experience.

Ingredients:

- 4 cloves

- 1 cinnamon stick

- 4 cups water

- 1-inch piece of fresh ginger, sliced

- 4 green cardamom pods, crushed

- 2 teaspoon loose black tea or 2 tea bags

- 1 cup milk (optional)

- 1 tbsp sugar or to taste

Method :

1. Bring the water to a boil in a pot.

2. Add the cloves, cinnamon stick, ginger, and cardamom pods. Simmer for 10 minutes.

3. Add the loose tea or tea bags and let it steep for 3-5 minutes.

4. Add milk and sugar, and bring the tea to a gentle boil. Steep 5 min and the masala chai is ready

5. Strain the tea into cups and serve hot.

## 8. DRIED BASIL AND CINNAMON TEA

Preparation and cooking time 20 minutes

Level : Easy

This tea combines the aromatic qualities of dried basil with the warm spice of cinnamon, making it a comforting choice.

Ingredients:

- 2 teaspoon dried basil leaves

- 1 cinnamon stick

- 4 cups water

- 2 Tea bags or 2 tsp loose black tea

- 1 tablespoon honey or sugar (optional)

Method :

1. Bring the water to a boil in a pot.

2. Add the dried basil leaves and cinnamon stick, and simmer for 7-10 minutes.

3. Add the loose tea or tea bags and steep for 3-5 minutes.

4. Strain the tea into cups, sweeten with honey or sugar if desired, and serve hot.

## 9. DRIED ROSE PETAL AND CARDAMOM TEA

Preparation and cooking time 20 minutes

Level : Easy

A delicate and floral tea that pairs the subtle sweetness of dried rose petals with the aromatic spice of cardamom.

Ingredients:

- 2 teaspoon clean dried rose petals

- 4 green cardamom pods, crushed

- 4 cups water

- 2 tea bags or 2 tsp loose black tea

- 1 tablespoon honey or sugar (optional)

Method :

1. Boil the water in a pot.

2. Add the dried rose petals and crushed cardamom pods, and let it simmer for 5 minutes.

3. Add the loose tea or tea bags and steep for 3-5 minutes.

4. Strain the tea into cups, sweeten with honey or sugar if desired, and serve hot.

10. MINT TEA

Preparation and cooking time 20 minutes

Level : Easy

A classic and refreshing tea made with just mint leaves, often enjoyed after meals in the Anglo Indian community

Ingredients:

- 2 teaspoons dried mint leaves

- 4 cups water

- 1 tablespoon honey or sugar (optional)

- Fresh mint leaves for garnish ( optional )

Method :

1. Bring the water to a boil in a pot.

2. Add the dried mint leaves and simmer for 5 minutes.

3. Remove from heat and let it steep for an additional 5 minutes.

4. Strain the tea into cups, sweeten with honey or sugar if desired, and garnish with fresh mint leaves. Serve hot or cold.

11. BAY LEAF TEA

Preparation and cooking time 20 minutes

A unique and aromatic tea made with bay leaves, known for its digestive properties.

Ingredients:

- 3 dried bay leaves

- 4 cups water

- 1 tbsp honey or sugar (optional)

- Lemon slices for garnish

Method :

1. Boil the water in a pot.

2. Add the dried bay leaves and simmer for 5-7 minutes.

3. Remove from heat and let it steep for an additional 5 minutes.

4. Strain the tea into cups, sweeten with honey or sugar if desired, and garnish with a lemon slice . Serve hot.

These teas offer a delightful combination of traditional Indian spices with the comforting qualities of Anglo-Indian tea culture. Enjoy them as a morning boost or an evening relaxer. These beverages are light, clear, and full of delicate flavors that can be enjoyed any time of the day.

Note : Be mindful if any individual allergies whensteeping these teas .

# CHAPTER TWELVE

# DINNER RECIPES

# 1. BEEF AND MUSHROOM IN WHITE SAUCE

Preparation and cooking time 45 min
Level : Medium Hard
Ingredients:

- 500 grams of bite sized beef cubes

- Small 200 grams can of sliced mushrooms

- Pinch of Dried herbs

- 1 onion chopped fine

- 2 garlic pods chopped or 1/2 teaspoon of garlic powder

- Salt and pepper

- 1 cup of milk or reconstituted milk

- 1 teaspoon of white flour

- 1 tablespoon butter

Method :

1.  Cook the beef until done . If pressure cooked ( 20 min ) . Pot cooked around 35 min . Reserve stock and keep aside .

1.  Melt butter add chopped onions and garlic , sauté until golden . Add cooked drained beef and drained mushrooms . Sauté on medium heat until lightly brown all over .

1.  Reduce heat and sprinkle the flour . Sauté two min and add the milk , a cup of reserved beef stock and a pinch of dried herbs .

1.  Reduce the liquid on low heat stirring so as not to burn , until gravy is thickened . Adjust salt and pepper .

1.  Serve with steamed rice , or flatbread , bun or slices of lightly toasted bread or rolls .

## 2. CRUSTY MINCE PIE

Preparation and cooking time 1 hour
Level : Hard
Ingredients:
For the Pie Crust:
- 2 cups all-purpose flour
- ½ cup cold butter, diced
- ½ teaspoon salt
- 4-6 tablespoons ice-cold water
For the Minced Meat Filling:
- 500g minced meat (beef, chicken or lamb )

- 1 onion, finely chopped
- 2 garlic cloves, minced or 1/2 teaspoon of its powder
- 1 tsp garam masala
- 2 tablespoons tomato paste or sauce
- ½ teaspoon turmeric powder
- ½ teaspoon paprika or red chili powder
- Salt and pepper to taste
- 2 tablespoon oil
- 2 tablespoons chopped fresh cilantro or 2 pinch of dried herbs (optional)
- 1 egg (for egg wash)

Method :

For the Pie Crust:

1. In a bowl, mix the flour and salt. Add the diced cold butter and rub it into the flour using your fingertips until the mixture resembles breadcrumbs.

2. Gradually add ice-cold water, 1 tablespoon at a time, and mix until the dough just comes together.

3. Form the dough into a ball, wrap it in plastic, and chill for 30 minutes.

For the Minced Meat Filling:

1. Heat the oil in a pan over medium heat. Add the chopped onion and cook until softened.

2. Add the garlic and tomato sauce and and sauté for another minute.

3. Stir in the minced meat, breaking it up with a spoon as it cooks. Cook until the meat is browned.

4. Add the garam masala, turmeric powder, paprika or red chili powder, salt, and pepper. Cook for 5 minutes until the meat is well-cooked and the spices are fragrant.

5. Stir in the herbs and remove from heat. Let the mixture cool.

Assemble and bake the Pie:

1. Preheat the oven to 190°C (375°F).

2. Roll out half of the chilled dough on a floured surface and line the bottom of a pie dish with it.

3. Spoon the minced meat filling evenly into the pie crust.

4. Roll out the remaining dough and place it over the filling. Seal the edges by pressing them together and crimping them with a fork or spoon .

5. Cut a few small slits in the top crust to allow steam to escape during baking.

6. Brush the top with an egg wash (1 egg mixed with 1 tablespoon water) for a golden crust.

7. Bake in the preheated oven for 30-40 minutes, or until the crust is golden brown and crispy.The time depends on your oven. Check occasionally , if done .

8. Let the pie cool for a few minutes before serving.

This Anglo-Indian Crusty Minced Meat Pie is simple and humble , yet full of flavor, and a comfort meal in itself .

Note : 1 tablespoon grated Cheddar or Parmesan cheese may be added to the filling , for extra cheesy flavor ( optional )


## 3. ANGLO INDIAN VERSION OF SHEPHERDS PIE WITH GRATED CHEESE

Preparation and cooking time 1 hour

Level : Hard

Ingredients:

For the Minced Meat Filling:

- 500g minced lamb or beef

- 1 onion, finely chopped

- 2 garlic cloves, minced or 1/2 teaspoon of its powder

- 1-inch ginger, grated or 1/2 teaspoon its powder

- 1/2 cup grated cheese

- 1 tsp garam masala
- ½ tsp turmeric powder


  - 1 large tomato, chopped
  - 1 tablespoon tomato paste or tomato sauce


- 1 cup mixed frozen vegetables (carrots, peas, or frozen broccoli with frozen cut beans )
- Salt and pepper to taste
- 2 tablespoons oil
- 2 tablespoons fresh cilantro or parsley or a pinch of dried herbs
- 1 tablespoon lemon juice

For the Mashed Potato Topping:
- 4 large potatoes, boiled and mashed
- 2 tablespoons butter
- ¼ cup milk
- Salt and pepper to taste
- 1 egg yolk (for browning)

Method :

For the Minced Meat Filling:

1. Heat oil in a pan over medium heat. Add the onions and sauté until golden brown.

2. Add the minced garlic, ginger, Cook for 1-2 minutes.

3. Add the minced meat and tomato paste or sauce and cook until browned, breaking up any lumps.

4. Stir in the garam masala, and turmeric. Cook the spices for 2-3 minutes until fragrant.

5. Add the chopped tomatoes and cook until they soften and blend into the meat.

6. Stir in the mixed vegetables, season with salt, pepper, and lemon juice. Cook for another 10 minutes until the vegetables are tender.

7. Add the cilantro or parsley , or the herbs and set the filling aside.

For the Mashed Potato Topping:

1. In a large bowl, mash the boiled potatoes with butter and milk until smooth and creamy.

2. Season with salt and pepper to taste.

1. Preheat the oven to 200°C (400°F).

2. Spread the minced meat filling evenly in a baking dish.

3. Spoon the mashed potatoes over the top and press and smooth it out to cover the meat completely.

4. Use a fork to press down the mashed potatoes evenly

5. Brush the top with egg yolk and sprinkle the grated cheese to give it a nice golden crust.

6. Bake in the preheated oven for 20 minutes or until the top is golden brown , cheese is melted and slightly crispy. Watch it , so it does not over crisp .

This Anglo-Indian Pie has the warmth of Indian spices combined with the comfort of creamy mashed potatoes, making it a hearty and flavorful comfort dish for dinner .


## 4. MEAT RICE

Preparation and cooking time 1 hour

Level : Medium hard

Ingredients :

- 500g Beef or Lamb cubed ( Can substitute with 500g mince Beef or Lamb for a lesser cooking time )

- 1 cup basmati rice

- 1 chopped onion

- 3 tablespoons oil or butter or ghee

- 1 tablespoon tomato paste or sauce
- 1/2 teaspoon black pepper powder
- 2 Sprigs of fresh cilantro or parsley chopped or two pinch of dried herbs

- 1/2 teaspoon cinnamon powder
- 1 teaspoon garam masala powder
- 1/2 teaspoon turmeric
- 1/2 cup of yoghurt or buttermilk

Method :

1. Steam or cook the rice with one tablespoon butter or oil and 2 cups of water and salt to taste , for 12-14 minutes until done and all the water is absorbed .

1. Sauté the chopped onion in the remaining oil or butter or ghee until translucent . Add the pepper powder , cinnamon powder , garam masala , turmeric , tomato paste or sauce and salt to taste . Sauté one minute .

2. Add the cubed beef or the mince . Sauté for five minutes in medium heat until the sauce is well coated and meat starts to brown slightly .

3. Add the Yoghurt or buttermilk and one cup of warm water and cook on low heat until done . They should not be any fluid left . If using beef cubes it takes approximately 25 minutes. If using mince it takes only 15 minutes . Add more warm water if the beef cubes are still not cooked . The mixture should be just moist with no visible fluid

4. Turn off the heat once cooked and add the sprigs of cilantro or parsley or the pinch of herbs . Toss in the steamed rice and fold in gently so that the beef and rice are well mixed but the rice does not get not broken . Rest

covered for five minutes.

5. Serve with any simple salad , tomato slices , pickle or just plain yoghurt .

## 5. HOME MADE TORTILLA ROLLED WITH OMELET

Preparation and cooking time 45 minutes

Level : Medium hard

Ingredients :

For tortilla :

- 1.5 cups of flour

- 1/2 teaspoon of salt

- Warm water 1/2 cup or as needed

-1 tablespoon oil

- 6 eggs

- 1/2 teaspoon black pepper powder

- 1 tablespoon tomato sauce or paste

- 1 small chopped onion

- Salt to taste

- A pinch of dried herbs ( optional )

- 2 tablespoon oil or butter

Method :

1. Add salt , oil and warm water to the flour . Knead five minutes to form a soft dough that can be rolled .

1. Cut into four portions . Roll out into circular shape .

2. Heat a non stick pan . Brush with a bit oil . Add tortilla until done on one side . Turn over and cook the other side . Make four tortillas one by one . Keep warm on a plate .

4. Beat the eggs with salt pepper and add the tomato paste and chopped onion . Heat oil or butter in a non stick pan and make four omelettes one by one . Each omelet should be approximately 1.5 egg batter

5. Place one omelet on each tortilla and roll up .

6. Serve drizzled with ketchup if needed .

Note : Grated Parmesan can be added to the egg batter for an extra flavor .


## 6. RICE OMLET

Preparation and cooking time

Level : Easy

Ingredients :

- 1/2 cup basmati rice or any soft rice

- 4 eggs beaten

- 1/2 teaspoon black pepper powder

- 1 tablespoon tomato paste or tomato sauce


- 1/4 teaspoon garlic powder ( optional )

- 3 tablespoons oil for frying the omlet

- 1 tablespoon butter for mashing the rice

- Salt to taste


Method :

1. Steam or cook the rice according to package instructions. If using basmati rice , it should be 2 cups water lightly salted for every cup of rice . In this case it should be one cup of water for the 1/2 cup of uncooked rice .When done and all water is absorbed . Add slightly more water if needed while cooking .

1. Mash the rice with a spoon with 1 tablespoon of butter while still hot . Keep aside .
2. Beat the eggs with pepper , tomato paste or sauce , and garlic powder , if using . Season with salt and pepper .
3. Heat oil or butter in a non stick pan . Make an omelet with half the beaten egg mixture and 1 tablespoon of oil Cook both sides on low heat until done . Place half the mashed rice on the center and fold the omelet .
4. Transfer to a plate complete the next omelet the same way .
5. Serve with a drizzle of ketchup ( optional )
6. Note : A teaspoon of grated Parmesan , may be added to the egg mixture for those who prefer it ( optional )

7. Pork Chops with Mustard Sauce:

Preparation and Cooking time 1 hour 30 min

Level : Hard

Ingredients:

- 6 pork chops, meat and fat
- 2 large onions, finely sliced
- 4 cloves garlic, minced or 1 teaspoon its powder
- 1 inch piece ginger, grated or 1/2 teaspoon its powder
- 2 tablespoon Dijon mustard or Anglo-Indian homemade mustard paste ( see below)
- 1 teaspoon turmeric powder
- 1 tsp black pepper, freshly ground
- 1/2 teaspoon paprika or red chili powder (optional)
- 1 cup milk or reconstituted coconut milk (optional)

- 2 tablespoon vinegar (white or malt)
- 1 tablespoon sugar

- tablespoons oil or ghee

- Salt to taste
- Fresh cilantro or parsley or a pinch of dried herbs for garnish
Method :

1. Marinate the Pork Chops by rubbing the pork chops with turmeric powder, black pepper, salt, and vinegar. Let them marinate for about 30 minutes to an hour.

2. Prepare the Mustard Paste in a grinder, by blending 2 teaspoon mustard seeds into a fine powder. If using homemade or store bought mustard paste, skip this step. Mix in the mustard paste with a little water to make a smooth sauce. Set aside.

3. Cook the Pork Chops by heating oil or ghee in a large skillet or heavy-bottomed pan. Sear the pork chops on both sides until they are browned and slightly crispy on the edges. Remove and set aside.

4. Prepare the Mustard Sauce by adding a little oil to the same pan, and sauté the sliced onions until they turn golden.

Add the minced garlic, ginger, or their powders , paprika or chili powder (if using), and sauté for another minute until fragrant.

Stir in the mustard paste and cook for 2-3 minutes.

Add sugar and milk or coconut milk (if using) to balance the flavors and bring the sauce together. Simmer for about 5 minutes, allowing the sauce to thicken slightly.

5. Return the seared pork chops to the pan, coating them well with the mustard sauce. Cover the pan and let the chops simmer in the sauce covered , for another 20 minutes on low heat until the meat is tender and the flavors are well absorbed . Check frequently so that it does not burn . This dish should be thick and moist with the sauce

6. Garnish with fresh chopped cilantro or parsley or the dried herbs and serve hot with steamed or roasted vegetables ( optional ) , steamed or cooked rice, warm bread, rolls or mashed potatoes.

This Anglo-Indian mustard pork chop recipe is a hot favorite among the community for celebrations and events and has a mild heat from the mustard with a tangy and slightly sweet finish, and is very typical of Anglo-Indian flavors.

## 8. PORK SORPOTEL

Preparation and cooking time 1 hour
Level : Hard
Pork Sorpotel (or Sorpotek) is a traditional Anglo-Indian dish with a rich, spicy, tangy flavor, rooted in Portuguese influence.
Ingredients:
500g pork shoulder or belly, cubed (fat and meat combined)
150g pork liver, cleaned and cubed (optional but traditional)

- 2 large onions, sliced
- 2 tablespoon tomato paste , tomato sauce or 2 tomatoes, chopped

- 8-10 garlic cloves, minced or 1 teaspoon of its powder
- 1-inch piece of ginger, grated or 1/2 teaspoon of its powder
- 1 tablespoon paprika or red chili powder
- 1 teaspoon black pepper powder
- 1 teaspoon turmeric powder
- 2 tablespoon vinegar
- 1 stick cinnamon or 1/2 teaspoon of its powder
- 4-5 cloves or 1/4 teaspoon of its powder
- 1 teaspoon garam masala
- 2 tablespoon oil

- Salt to taste
- 1/2 cup water
- 1 tablespoon sugar (optional, to balance flavors)
Method :

1.  Prepare the Pork by Boiling the pork (including the liver) in water with some salt and turmeric powder.

1.  After boiling, drain and cut the meat and liver into smaller bite size pieces .Save the stock for later use.

3. Sear the Pork by Heating oil in a large pan or skillet. Fry the boiled pork and liver until lightly browned and crispy on the edges. Set aside.

4. In the same pan, add sliced onions and sauté until golden brown.

5. Add the all ground spices and two tablespoons of water and cook for about 5 minutes on low heat until the oil separates from the sauce .

6. Add the chopped tomatoes or the tomato paste or sauce and cook until they soften and combine well with the spices. Add the browned pork and liver to the pan, mixing thoroughly so that the meat is well coated with the masala.

7. Add the saved pork stock or water to the pan, with the vinegar , bring to a boil, and then reduce the heat to a simmer. Cover and cook for about 40 minutes until the meat is tender and the sauce has thickened. Check frequently if burning .

8. Add sugar if using to balance out the tanginess and heat. Adjust seasoning with salt and vinegar if needed.

Sorpotel is one of those dishes that tastes better the next day as the flavors develop. So it tastes best when you allow it to rest two days in the refrigerator before reheating and serving.

7. Serve hot with steamed rice, warm rolls , flatbread or bread.

This Anglo-Indian version of Pork Sorpotel is full of spice and flavor with an option for adding liver, which gives it a traditional depth .

# CHAPTER THIRTEEN
# JAMS AND PRESERVES

### 1. MIXED FRUIT JAM

Preparation and cooking time 1 hour

Level : Hard

Ingredients:

- 1 cup pineapple, cleaned and diced
- 1 cup mango, diced
- 1 cup apple, peeled and diced
- 1 cup papaya or guava, diced and deseeded
- 2 cups sugar
- 1/4 cup lemon juice
- 1/2 teaspoon ground cinnamon (optional)
- 1/4 teaspoon salt

Method:

1. Peel, dice, and blend the fruits separately to make smooth purees or use a combination of diced and pureed fruits for texture of a preserve .

2. In a heavy-bottomed pan, combine all the blended fruits and cook the puréed fruit mixture , sugar, and salt. Cook over medium heat, stirring frequently to prevent burning.

3. When the mixture starts to thicken (about 20 minutes), add lemon juice and the optional spices (cinnamon powder if using ). Continue to cook, on low heat , stirring often, until the jam reaches a thick, gel-like consistency that coats the spoon thickly . This may take an additional 15 minutes.

4. To test if the jam is ready, and the consistency place a small amount on a cold plate and let it cool. Run your finger through the jam; if it holds its shape and wrinkles slightly, it's done.

5. Remove from heat and let the jam cool slightly before transferring it to sterilized jars. Seal the jars while still warm and let them cool completely before storing preferably in the refrigerator. Use within a month .

This mixed fruit jam is delicious on buns and toast or as a topping for other desserts like tarts , pies or biscuits

## 2. WATERMELON / BLACK GRAPE JAM FUSION RECIPE

Preparation and cooking time. Freeze time 1 hour . Cooking time 40 minutes

Level : Medium hard

Ingredients:

- 4 cups watermelon, deseeded and chopped
- 2 cups black grapes, seedless freeze for one hour in a bag
- 2 cups sugar (adjust based on sweetness )
- 2 tablespoons lemon juice
- 1 teaspoon grated ginger (optional)
- 1 tsp butter (to reduce foam while cooking )

Method:

1. Blend the watermelon until smooth. Blend the chilled grapes until creamy . Strain in a wide strainer if you notice seeds , for a smoother texture. Do not strain if you need some texture.

2. Cook the fruit in a large saucepan, add both the watermelon puree and black grapes. Bring to a simmer on medium heat, stirring occasionally.

3. Once the fruit has softened, add the sugar and stir continuously until it dissolves. You'll notice the mixture becoming thick and glossy.

4. Stir in the lemon juice now to balance the sweetness and help with preservation. If using ginger, add it now for an aromatic touch.

5. Keep stirring the jam on medium heat as it boils. You can add butter at this point to reduce foam if needed . Cook until the jam reaches a gel type consistency. This could take around 30 minutes.

6. To test and check if the jam is ready, drop a little on a cold plate. It should coat the stirring spoon thickly . If it sets and wrinkles on the plate when touched, then it's done.

7. Once done, let the jam cool slightly. Transfer into sterilized jars and store in the refrigerator. Use within two months .

This jam is sweet, bursting with fruity flavors, and pairs wonderfully with bread, bun , or can be used to make flavored yogurt! This sweet Anglo-Indian watermelon and black grape jam is a delightful blend of two summer fruits.

# 3. APPLE AND PINEAPPLE JAM

Preparation and cooking time 50 minutes

Level : Medium hard

Ingredients:

- 3 cups apples (peeled, cored, and chopped)
- 2 cups pineapple (use fresh or canned, chopped)
- 3 cups sugar (adjust to your need)
- 2 tablespoon lemon juice

- 1 teaspoon grated ginger ( optional )

- 1/2 cup warm water

Method:

1. Peel, core, and chop the apples into small cubes. For the pineapple, finely chop the fruit, ensuring there are no inedible bits. Pulse them both lightly in a blender if you prefer creamier texture .

2.In a large saucepan, add the chopped apples or blended and water. Cook over medium heat until the apples soften, about 10 minutes, stirring occasionally.

3. Once the apples are softened, add the chopped or blended pineapple and grated ginger (if using). Continue to cook the mixture for another 10 minutes until the pineapple softens and blends with the apples.

4. Stir in the sugar and lemon juice. Increase the heat a bit and bring the mixture to a boil. Stir continuously in medium heat to dissolve the sugar and prevent the jam from sticking to the bottom.

5. Boil the jam until reduced and thick but fluid , stirring frequently, until it reaches a thick, jammy consistency. It should coat the spoon. This should take around 25 minutes.

6. To check if the jam is set, place a small spoonful on a cold plate and let it cool. If it forms like a gel and wrinkles when touched, the jam is ready.

7. Once done, remove from heat and let it cool slightly. Pour the jam into sterilized jars, leaving a little space at the top. Seal the jars and store in the refrigerator. Use it within two months .

This Anglo-Indian-inspired apple and pineapple jam combines the sweetness of apples with the tropical tang of pineapple, creating a delicious spread with a balanced sweetness and tropical hue . Serve it on pancakes or buns or toasted bread . Suitable also as sweet meat glaze instead of honey .

## 4 . ANGLO INDIAN ORANGE MARMALADE ( MANDARIN) WITH PEEL

Preparation and cooking time 50 minutes

Level : Medium hard

Ingredients:

- 8-10 medium-sized mandarin oranges (about 4 cups of fruit)

- 1 mandarin worth of peel (adjust this to your preference)

- 4 cups sugar

- 2 tbsp lemon juice

- 2 cups water

Method:

1. Peel the mandarins, and set aside a few peels (from 1 orange). Remove as much of the white pith as possible from the peels, or the marmalade will be bitter. Slice the peels into thin strips or small bits, as your preference for texture .

2. Segment the mandarins and remove seeds. Cut the fruit into small chunks or blend lightly for a smoother marmalade according to your preference

3. In a small saucepan, add the peel strips and cover with water. Bring to a boil and cook for about 5 minutes to soften them and remove any bitterness. Drain and set aside.

4. In a large pot, combine the mandarin chunks (and their juice, if any) with 2 cups of water. Add the drained boiled peel strips and bring the mixture to a boil over medium heat. Simmer for about 15 minutes, stirring occasionally.

5. After the fruit has softened, stir in the sugar and lemon juice. Continue to cook the mixture, stirring frequently, on medium heat until the sugar has dissolved.

6. Increase the heat slightly and let the marmalade boil, stirring regularly to avoid sticking. The mixture will begin to thicken after 30 minutes.

7. To check if the marmalade has set, place a small spoonful on a cold plate and let it cool for a minute. If it wrinkles when pushed, it's ready. If not, cook for a little longer. It should coat the spoon thickly .

8. Remove the pot from heat and allow the marmalade to cool slightly. Pour it into sterilized jars, leaving a little space at the top. Seal tightly and store in the fridge.Use within two months

This is an Anglo-Indian-style mandarin orange marmalade , encompassing sweet tart flavors of bursting citrus zest with a few bits of orange peel for that delightful lovely chew and citrusy bite . Serve on buns flatbreads , toasted bread or even use it as a glaze for poultry .

# CHAPTER FOURTEEN
# ANGLO INDIAN AND FUSION PICKLES

A few Anglo-Indian recipes for pickles that bring together a fusion of Indian spices and British flavors:

1. **MIXED VEGETABLE PICKLE**

1. Preparation and cooking time 45 minutes
2. Level : Medium hard

Ingredients:

- 2 cups of assorted vegetables (carrot, cauliflower, whole green olives or whole black olives , ( optional ) turnip or radish , green whole long chili , ten pods peeled whole garlic )
- 1 cup white vinegar
- 1 tablespoon mustard
- 1 teaspoon turmeric powder
- 1 teaspoon chili powder or paprika
- 2 tablespoon ginger-garlic paste or 1 teaspoon each of their powders
- 1/2 cup mustard oil or olive oil
- Salt to taste
- 2 tablespoon sugar

Method :

1. Wash and chop the vegetables into small pieces.

2. Boil or steam the vegetables with salt to taste until half-cooked. Drain and dry on paper napkin

3. Heat mustard oil in a pan in low heat

4. Add ginger-garlic paste, or their powders , turmeric powder, and chili or paprika powder. Fry for a minute. Add mustard .

5. Add the vegetables, vinegar, sugar, and salt. Cook on low heat for 10 minutes.

6. Allow the pickle to cool before storing it in an airtight jar in the refrigerator And use within two months .


## 2. EGGPLANT PICKLE

Marinade : 30 minutes . Preparation and cooking time 30 minutes

Level : Medium hard

Ingredients:

- 500g eggplants chopped
- 1 cup white vinegar
- 1 tablespoon mustard
- 1 tablespoon fenugreek seeds
- 1 teaspoon turmeric powder
- 1 teaspoon paprika or chili powder
- 1/2 cup mustard oil or olive oil
- Salt to taste
- 2 tablespoon sugar

Method :

1. Sprinkle salt on chopped eggplant and let them sit for 30 minutes. Rinse and pat dry or dry on paper napkin .

2. Heat mustard oil or olive oil and add fenugreek seeds or their powder . Let them crackle.

3. Add the chopped eggplant turmeric, and paprika or chili powder . Fry until they soften.

4. Add vinegar and sugar, then cook for another 10 minutes.

5. Cool and store in a sterilized jar in the refrigerator. Use within a month .

### 3. LIME AND GINGER PICKLE

Marinade : Overnight . Preparation and cooking time 30 minutes

Level : Medium hard

Ingredients:

- 10 small limes, halved or quartered
- 1 cup grated fresh ginger or 2 teaspoons of ginger powder
- 1 cup sugar
- 1 cup white vinegar
- 1 teaspoon mustard
- 1 teaspoon turmeric powder
- 1 teaspoon paprika or chili powder
- 1/2 cup mustard oil or olive oil

- Salt to taste

Method :

1. Combine sliced limes and grated or powdered ginger in a bowl with salt, turmeric, and paprika or chili powder . Let it sit overnight.

2. Heat mustard oil or olive oil in a pan, on low heat

3. Add the lime-ginger mixture, sugar, and vinegar.

4. Cook in low heat until the limes become soft and the mixture thickens.

5. Cool and transfer to a jar . Store in the refrigerator and use within two months .

### 4. MANGO PICKLE

Marinade 2 hours Preparation and cooking time 30 minutes

Level Medium hard

Ingredients:

- 4 raw mangoes, peeled deseeded and sliced

- 1 cup sugar

- 1/2 cup white vinegar

- 1 tablespoon sugar

- 1 tablespoon mustard

- 1 teaspoon paprika or chili powder

- 1 teaspoon turmeric powder

- 1/2 cup mustard oil or olive oil


- Salt to taste

Method :

1. Mix mango slices with salt, turmeric, and chili powder. Let it sit for 2 hours.

2. Heat mustard oil, on low heat

3. Add the mango slices, sugar, and vinegar.

4. Cook on low heat until the mangoes are soft and the mixture becomes syrupy.

5. Cool and store in a jar in the refrigerator and use within two months .

These recipes offer a delicious blend of fusion flavors that are characteristic of Anglo-Indian cuisine, perfect for adding a tangy and spicy twist to your main meals.

CHAPTER FIFTEEN
FRUIT PUNCH ( mildly alcoholic )
MIXED FRUIT PUNCH
**Prep time 2 hours**
Level : Hard
Anglo-Indian-style Mixed Fruit Punch / Wine
Ingredients:
- 1 cup pineapple chopped
- 1 cup chopped apples
- 2 cups grapes deseeded
- 1/2 cup pomegranate seeds ( optional for color , flavor )
- 1 cup sugar ( can be adjusted more or less according to preference )
- 1 lemon, juiced

- 1/2 teaspoon yeast (wine or bread yeast)
- 4 whole cloves ( optional for flavor )

- 4 cups clean drinkable water or bottled water
Instructions:

1. Prepare all the fruits and chop them . Do not remove skins . Mash the fruits with a spoon for 15 minutes with a little water if needed. Add the lemon juice

2. In a large steel or glass pot with a lid , combine all the mashed fruits , sugar and yeast , cloves if using , and 4 cups of clean water. The pot or container should be only half filled

3. Mix gently and close the lid ( loosely ) . It's very important that the lid should not be tightened . It should be just placed in a way that insects can't get in . Alternatively you can place a clean dry kitchen towel instead of a lid and loosely tie with a string

4 . Allow the mixture to cool and ferment for 4 days at room temperature.

5. Stir gently , daily only once

6. On the fourth day , strain the mixture through a fine mesh strainer or cheesecloth into clean bottles, leaving some space at the top.

7. Close the bottles without tightening and store in refrigerator.

8. After 24 hours , strain them again , only if you see sediment .

9. Use within the week and Chill before serving. It may be served in 100 ml portions only . The punch will be mildly alcoholic due to the fermentation and have a pleasant sweet flavor. This punch should be used only by adults .


## SWEET CASHEW FRUIT PUNCH
### ( STRONG , ONLY FOR ADULT CONSUMPTION )
Preparation time 2 hours
Level : Hard


Ingredients:
- 10-12 ripe cashew fruits (cashew apples)
- 1 cup sugar (adjust more or less according to preference )
- 1 lemon, juiced
- 1/2 teaspoon wine yeast (or bread yeast )
- 4 cups clean drinkable water or bottled water

Method :

1. Prepare the cashew fruits by washing them thoroughly and cut them into pieces.

2. Juice the fruit by blending the cashew fruit pieces lightly , to extract the juice. Use a strainer or cheesecloth to separate the juice from the pulp.

3. Mix the cashew fruit juice and water In a large pot

Stir in the sugar and lemon juice until the sugar is completely dissolved. The pot should be only half filled

4. Allow the mixture to cool to room temperature.

Sprinkle the yeast on top for fermentation and stir gently to combine.

Cover the pot with a clean cloth not a lid and let it ferment in a warm place for 5 days. Stir daily , gently , only once .

5. After fermentation, strain the mixture through a fine mesh strainer or cheesecloth into clean bottles, leaving some space at the top.

Next day strain the juice again, only if you notice sediment . Seal the bottles but not tightly and let them age for about 1 week in a refrigerator and serve only for adults in 100 ml portions . It's a very strong tasting punch .

6. Chill before serving. The wine should be sweet with a fruity flavor from the cashew fruit and should be served along with food . It's mildly alcoholic due to fermentation .


## 3. SWEET RED GRAPE PUNCH

Preparation time 2 hours

Level : Hard

Ingredients:

- 3 lbs (about 1.4 kg) red grapes

- 2 cups sugar (adjust more or less to preference)

- 1 lemon, juiced

- 1/2 teaspoon wine yeast (or bread yeast )

- 4 cups clean drinkable water or bottled water

Method :

1. Prepare and wash the grapes thoroughly and remove stems.

Crush the grapes gently with the back of a spoon to release their juice. You can do this by hand or using a grape crusher or a few spurts only in a blender . Do not grind.

2. Transfer the crushed grapes, including the skins, to a large pot.

Add 2 cups of water and heat gently to help extract more juice. Do not boil. Stir occasionally and mash the grapes further if needed.

Allow the mixture to cool to room temperature.

3.Strain the mixture through a fine mesh strainer or cheesecloth into a clean container, pressing to extract as much juice as possible.

Add the remaining 2 cups of water to the juice.

Stir in the sugar and lemon juice until the sugar is completely dissolved.

4. Sprinkle the yeast on top of the mixture and stir gently.

Cover the container with a clean cloth and let it ferment in a warm place for about 5 days. Stir daily , gently , only once .

5. Strain and bottle the punch on the fifth day after fermentation, into clean bottles, leaving some space at the top. Next day strain again only if you notice sediment

Seal the bottles by capping them( not so tight ) and let them age in a refrigerator for ten days . It can be kept up to two months .

6. Chill before serving. Serve only for adults as it is mildly alcoholic due to the fermentation. The wine will be sweet with a rich, fruity flavor.

# EPILOGUE

This book has sought to bring you closer to the authenticity of Anglo-Indian food. Whether it's the sweet and savory delights of fried Saviling or the robust flavors of Ball Curry, these dishes embody a history of resilience, adaptation, and nostalgia. Every meal carries a story—perhaps of a family gathered around a table, a kitchen filled with the scent of freshly ground spices, or the warmth of a housekeeper or grandmother's hands . Each recipe is a tribute to the Anglo-Indian communities that have preserved these traditions while they survived on strange host country soil

This is not just a book for those with deep roots in the Anglo-Indian diaspora. The recipes have been designed for all to enjoy—those familiar with the cuisine and those discovering it for the first time. By using readily available ingredients and offering practical substitutions, I hope this book encourages you to experiment in your own kitchen . After all, food is meant to be shared, enjoyed, and passed down, connecting generations and transcending boundaries.

In writing this book, the goal was to honor the food that shaped a childhood and still continues to inspire . I hope these recipes bring as much joy to your home as they have to the Anglo Indian community . Beyond the measurements and instructions, I encourage you to explore, adjust, and make each dish your own. As with any good recipe, it's not just about following the steps—it's about creating memories and forging connections with those who share your table.

Thank you for joining me on this flavorful journey through time, culture, and cuisine. May the meals you create from these pages nourish not only your body but also your soul, keeping the spirit of Anglo-Indian cooking alive for generations to come.

# About the Author

The author , Ms. Mendez , is of Portuguese ancestry and Anglo Indian origin . She holds a Masters in Aviation from Switzerland , and currently lives in Kuwait . The author can be reached on email : hellorishimendez@gmail.com

Caption

# Also by Rishi Mendez


Breaking Free
It Wasn't Just You
Kuwait The Tiny But Mighty Kingdom
AUTHENTIC Anglo Indian Recipes